TEACH YOURSELF TO PLAY

UKULELE

by Doug Boduch

ISBN 978-1-7051-3519-8

HAL•LEONARD®
A Muse Group Company

I0805573

Visit Hal Leonard Online at
www.halleonard.com

World headquarters, contact:
Hal Leonard
7777 West Bluemound Road
Milwaukee, WI 53213
Email: info@halleonard.com

In Europe, contact:
Hal Leonard Europe Limited
Dettingen Way
Bury St Edmunds, Suffolk, IP33 3YB
Email: info@halleonardeurope.com

In Australia, contact:
Hal Leonard Australia Pty. Ltd.
4 Lentara Court
Cheltenham, Victoria, 3192 Australia
Email: info@halleonard.com.au

Introduction

Congratulations on your decision to play the ukulele! It's a super fun and easy instrument to play, and this book will be perfect to help you start your musical journey. The goal of this book is to get you playing quickly, so you won't have to learn to read standard music notation. The music is presented instead in an easy-to-learn format called tablature (or tab), a system of notating music that can be learned almost instantly. In other words, you can start right now!

We'll begin by learning about the parts of the ukulele and how to hold the instrument. Then, we'll start playing some simple melodies, learning the easy tablature notation system as we go. After that, we'll learn a few chords and strum some popular songs. While musical terms and concepts will be discussed, the main focus will be on playing. Even though we'll take a fast-and-easy approach to the uke, by the end of the book, you'll be playing some great-sounding arrangements.

The objective of the book is not only to get you on the path to learning the instrument right away, but also to promote continued learning after you've completed the book. All the fundamentals you'll learn will set a solid foundation for you to build upon later. With a musical instrument, you never stop learning—you just find harder songs to play!

To get the most out of this book, take your time and enjoy the journey. Resist the urge to rush through any material, and always feel free to review or spend extra time on anything that gives you trouble. You'll need to be not only the student but also the teacher. So, listen closely to what you're playing and don't move on until you feel comfortable with whatever it is you're working on. As far as practice time, it's better to put in multiple short sessions than to do one monster practice session on the weekend, so aim to pick up the uke most days of the week. Even practicing 15 minutes, twice a day, will pay dividends. Try to leave your uke in a place where you can easily grab it and get a quick practice session in.

Chapter 1
Getting Started

Parts of the Ukulele

Ukuleles come in many shapes and sizes, but they all share the same parts. Take a look at the following picture and become acquainted with the names of the parts, as we'll be using many of these names throughout the book.

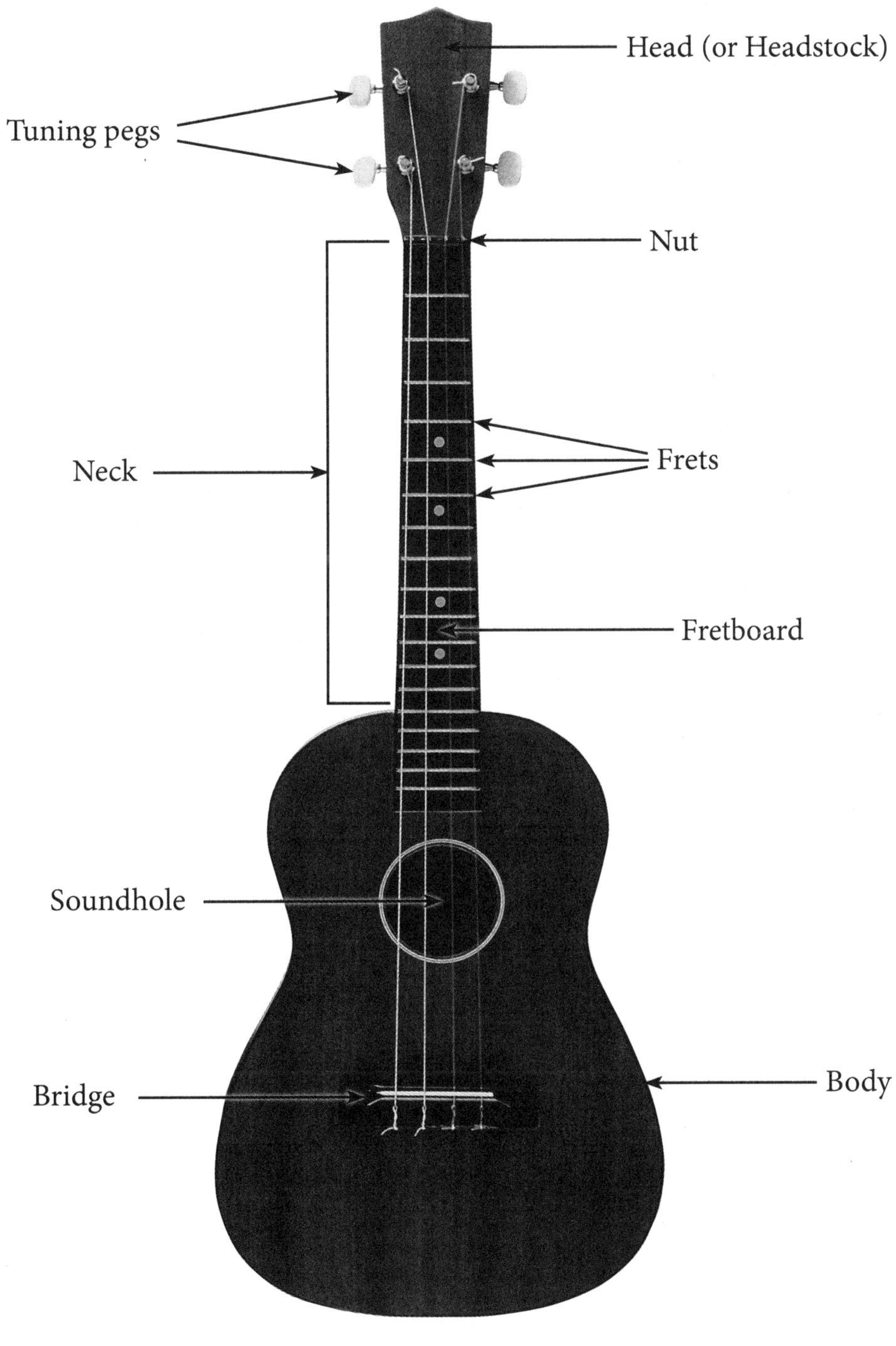

How to Hold the Ukulele

There are a few ways that you can hold your ukulele, but the seated position is perhaps the most popular. Simply rest the instrument on your right leg and apply a small amount of pressure with your right forearm to keep the uke stable against your body.

The standing position puts the instrument in the same general location against your body, but a little more pressure from your right forearm is required to keep it in place.

If you prefer to stand, you might want to try using a *strap*, because it can help hold the uke in place better. Straps are made to go over your shoulder or around your neck. Check to see whether or not your ukulele includes strap buttons to attach a strap to the instrument, as shown in the first photo. If not, these can be installed by a professional, or you can choose a strap style that doesn't require strap buttons, as shown in the second photo with the strap strung around the body of the uke and connected to the soundhole.

Left-Hand Technique

The left-hand fingers will do the *fretting*, the basic technique of using the fingers to press down on the strings. You'll get the best sound when fretting if you always press down the strings right behind the frets. Try to keep your thumb behind the neck and be sure to arch your fingers, touching only the fingertips to the strings. We number the fingers of the left hand 1 through 4: 1 = index, 2 = middle, 3 = ring, and 4 = pinky.

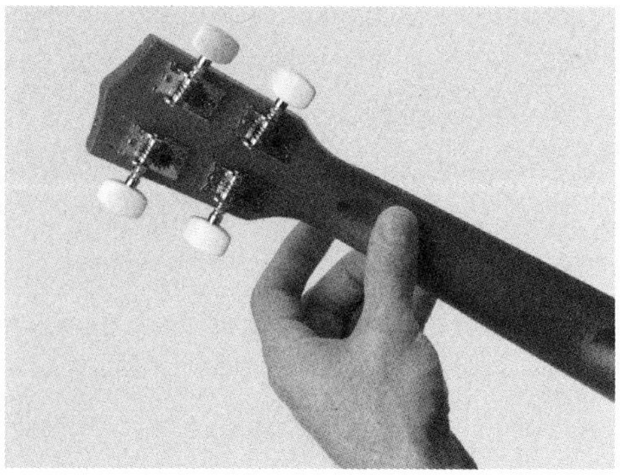

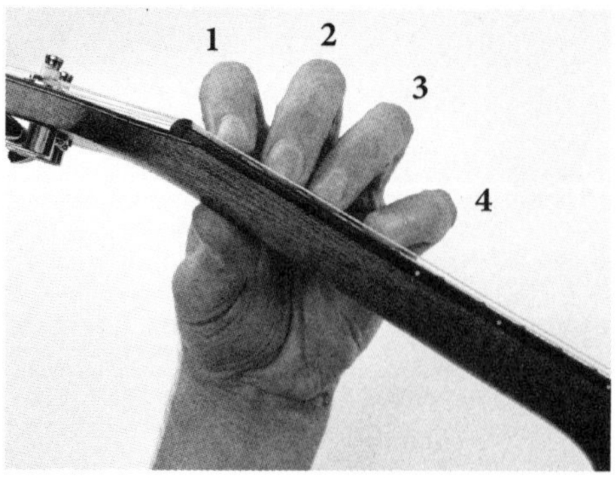

Right-Hand Technique

Our right-hand technique will differ depending on what we're doing. When playing single notes, most players will pluck in a downward motion with the thumb. You can also try plucking upwards with the first or second finger. For strumming, position the right hand over the spot where the neck joins the body and aim for strumming or plucking the strings in that area. We can strum with the thumb alone, with the first finger, with the thumb and first finger together, or with a *pick*. If you'd like to try using a pick, keep in mind that most uke players use a thick felt pick, as it produces a warm, clear sound.

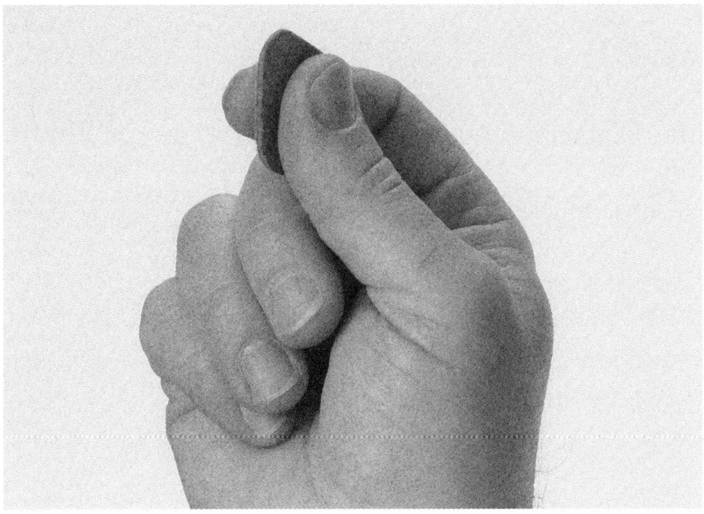

String Pitches and Tuning

Before we start playing, you'll want to tune your ukulele. If you tighten a tuning peg, it will raise the *pitch* (the highness or lowness) of the string. Conversely, if you loosen a tuning peg, it will lower the pitch of the string. The strings of the ukulele are numbered 1 through 4, with 1 being closest to the floor and 4 being closest to your chest. The pitches of the strings are as follows: 1 = A, 2 = E, 3 = C, 4 = G. While there are many ways to tune, by far the easiest is with an electronic tuner. If you don't have one, you can use a free online tuner or download an app for your phone. Eventually, you'll develop a musical ear and will be able to tune just by listening to the strings—but for now, the tuner will be your friend!

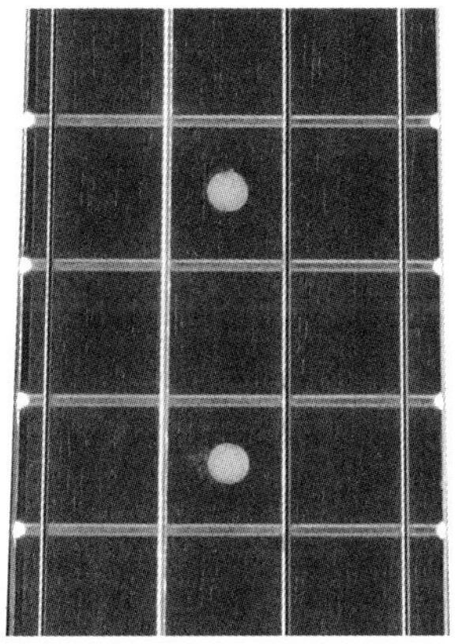

string name: G C E A
string number: 4 3 2 1

How to Practice

Learning a musical instrument like the ukulele takes time and effort. Be patient and progress will come. Try to fit in some time each day to play the ukulele. It's much better to get in 30 minutes every day than to save up all your practice time for the weekends. There's nothing wrong with doing a two-hour mega-practice session, but repeated daily practice is the real key to improvement. And repetition is the key to practice. Many times, it will be helpful to just repeat some small sections of a song rather than to work on the entire thing all at once. Above all, have fun and enjoy the journey!

Chapter 2

Playing Melodies on the First Two Strings

Reading Tablature

In this book, we'll use a popular system of notation known as *tablature* (or *tab*). With tab, you'll see four lines that represent the four strings of the ukulele. The line on top represents string 1, the string that's closest to the floor when holding your ukulele. If you pluck that string *open*, meaning you're not using your left hand at all to fret any of the strings, you'll be playing your first note, an A.

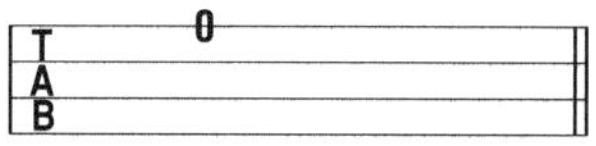

Notice that in the last tab we used a "0" (zero) on string 1 to indicate that it's played open. When we need to use a finger on the left hand to fret a note on a certain string, a number other than zero will be placed on the appropriate line in the tab to represent the fret number to be played. Let's try fretting a note on string 2. Place finger 3 (ring finger) just behind the 3rd fret to play a G on string 2.

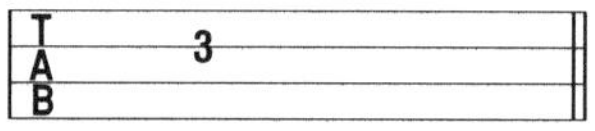

If a fretted note sounds muffled, make sure that you're not too close to the fret (or too far away from it) and that you're using enough pressure. Keep the thumb behind the neck to add support. Now, let's use finger 1 (index) to play an F on the 1st fret of string 2.

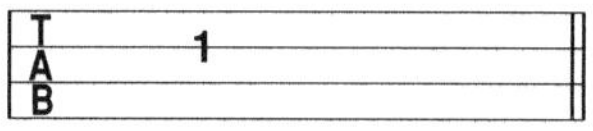

One more note to learn and we can play our first melody! Use finger 3 on the 3rd fret of string 1 to play a C.

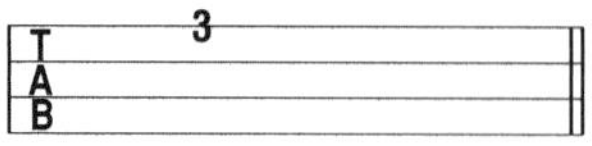

Once the first four notes are sounding good, we can put them together and play our first song, "Mary Had a Little Lamb." Simply pluck the respective note when you see the tab number. Pay close attention to which string the number is on!

Mary Had a Little Lamb

Words by Sarah Josepha Hale
Traditional Music

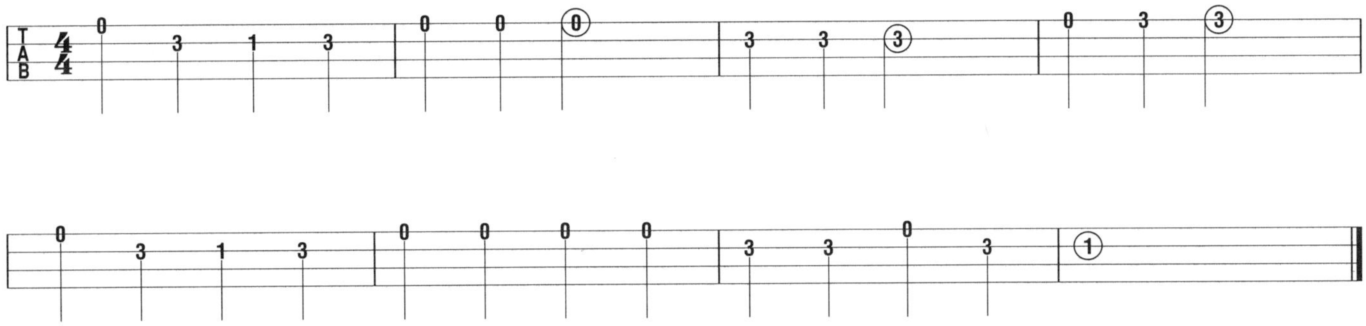

Note Values

Most likely, you played the last melody correctly without even thinking about how long each note lasts! But did you notice the vertical lines underneath the tab numbers? And why were some numbers circled? Well, to represent the *duration* of each note, or how long each particular note lasts, we need to add lines and circles to the tab numbers. The notes with just a line attached are called *quarter notes*, and they receive one beat. When you count off a song ("one, two, three, four") or tap your foot, you're counting quarter notes. The circled notes with a line are called *half notes*, and they receive two beats. So, a single half note lasts twice as long as a quarter note. Finally, the last note value we'll learn for now, just a circled number without a line, is called a *whole note*, and this type of note is worth four beats.

Let's learn one more note on the fretboard and play another popular melody. For this note, B♭ (pronounced B-flat), place finger 1 on the 1st fret of string 1.

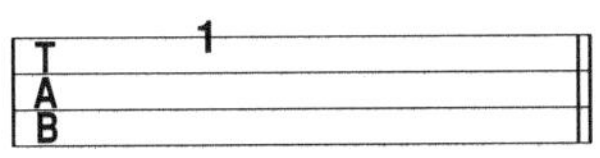

Jingle Bells

Words and Music by J. Pierpont

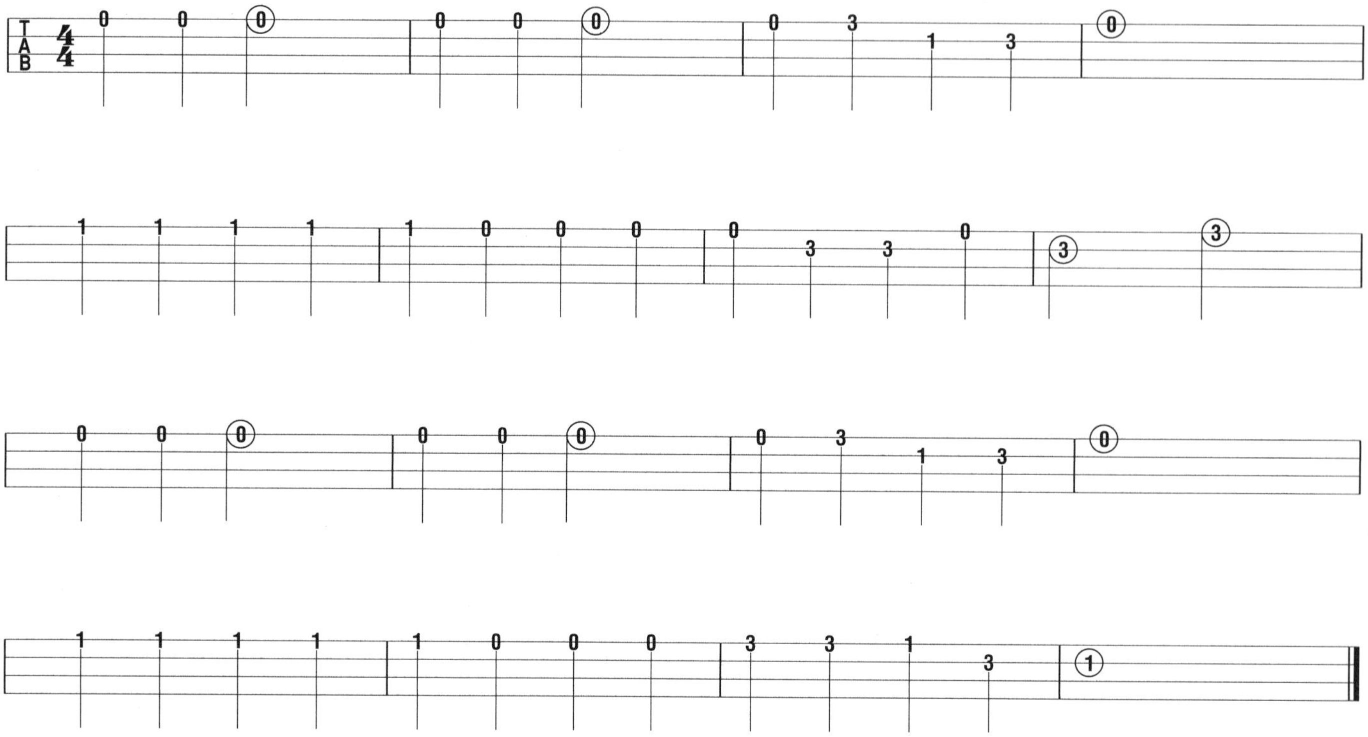

If you're wondering what that "♭" symbol means, it's part of a group of musical symbols called ***accidentals****, which lower or raise a note. The "♭" is called a* ***flat****, and it lowers any note by one fret. Conversely, a* ***sharp*** *(♯) raises the pitch of any note by one fret. Remember, notes get lower in pitch as you move towards the tuning pegs, and higher in pitch as you approach the bridge.*

Speaking of higher notes, let's learn the D on the 5th fret of string 1. You can use either finger 3 or finger 4 (pinky) to fret the note.

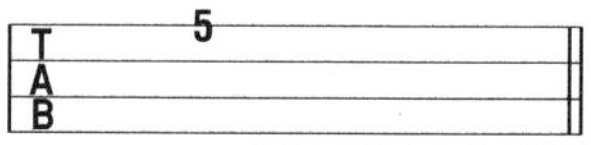

Now that we know the D on string 1, we can play "Twinkle, Twinkle Little Star."

Twinkle, Twinkle Little Star

Traditional

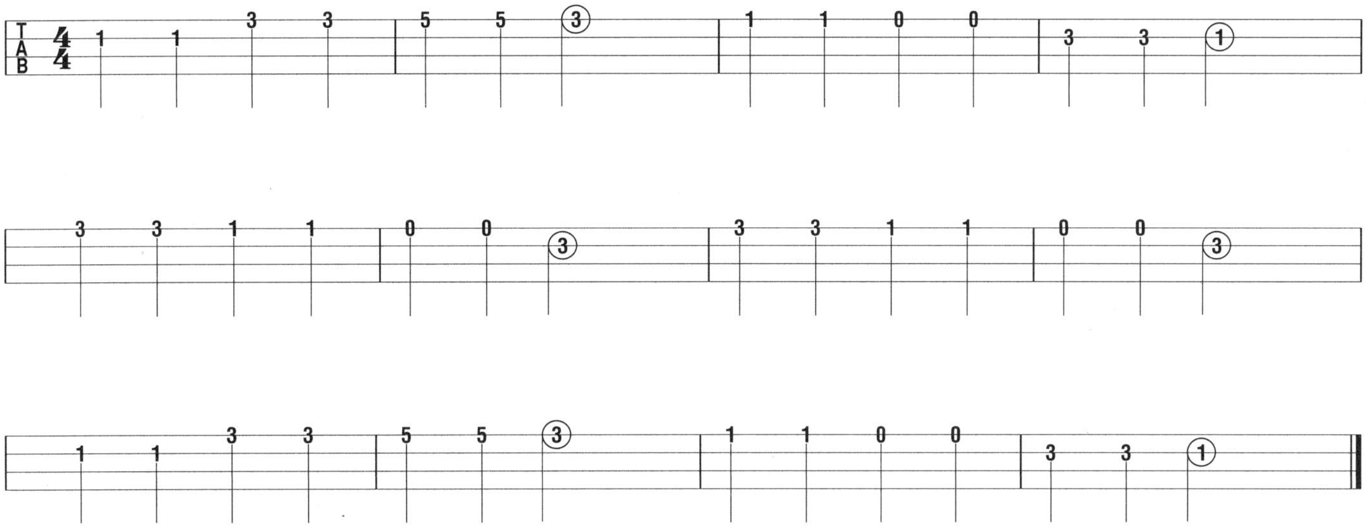

4/4 Time Signature

You may have noticed that each song we played so far began with the numbers 4/4 (pronounced "four-four"). This is called a *time signature*, and one will always appear at the beginning of a piece of music. The vertical lines running through the four horizontal lines separate the music into what are called *measures* (or *bars*) that each contain the same number of beats, and a time signature tells us how many beats are in each of these measures. When you see a *4/4 time signature*, it means you'll have four beats in each measure, and the quarter note will be counted as one beat. The top number always tells us how many beats are in each measure, while the bottom number tells us what type of note gets counted as one beat.

Here's another popular song we can play with the notes we've learned so far. Notice that we again have a 4/4 time signature. It can be helpful to count along as you play, counting "one, two, three, four" for each measure.

Go Tell Aunt Rhody

Traditional

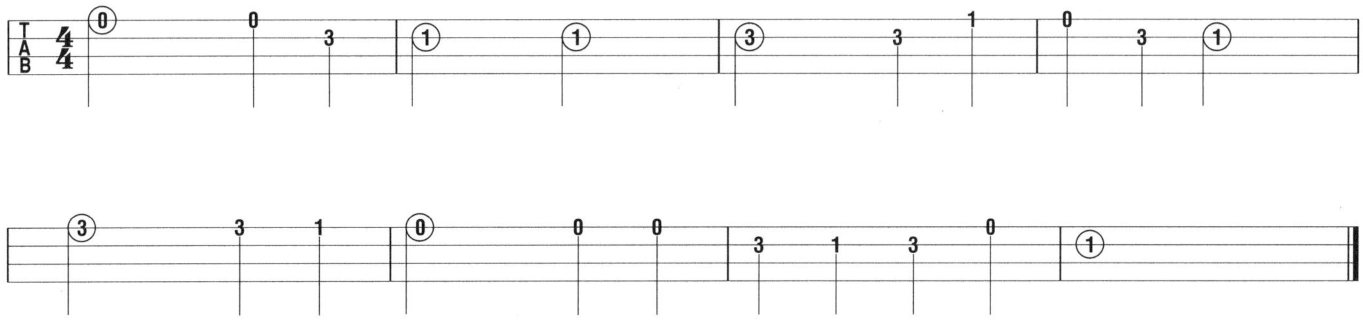

Pick-up Notes

Sometimes a song will begin with one or more *pick-up notes*. In other words, the melody doesn't start on beat one of the first measure. The extra note(s) are shown in an incomplete measure at the start called a *pick-up measure*. So, to make sure you come in on the right beat, just silently count the missing beats at the beginning before playing the pick-up note(s).

"Oh! Susanna" includes one pick-up note: a quarter note on beat four of the pick-up measure. So, since we're missing beats one, two, and three in the pick-up measure, you'll count "one, two, three" and come in on beat four.

Oh! Susanna

Words and Music by Stephen C. Foster

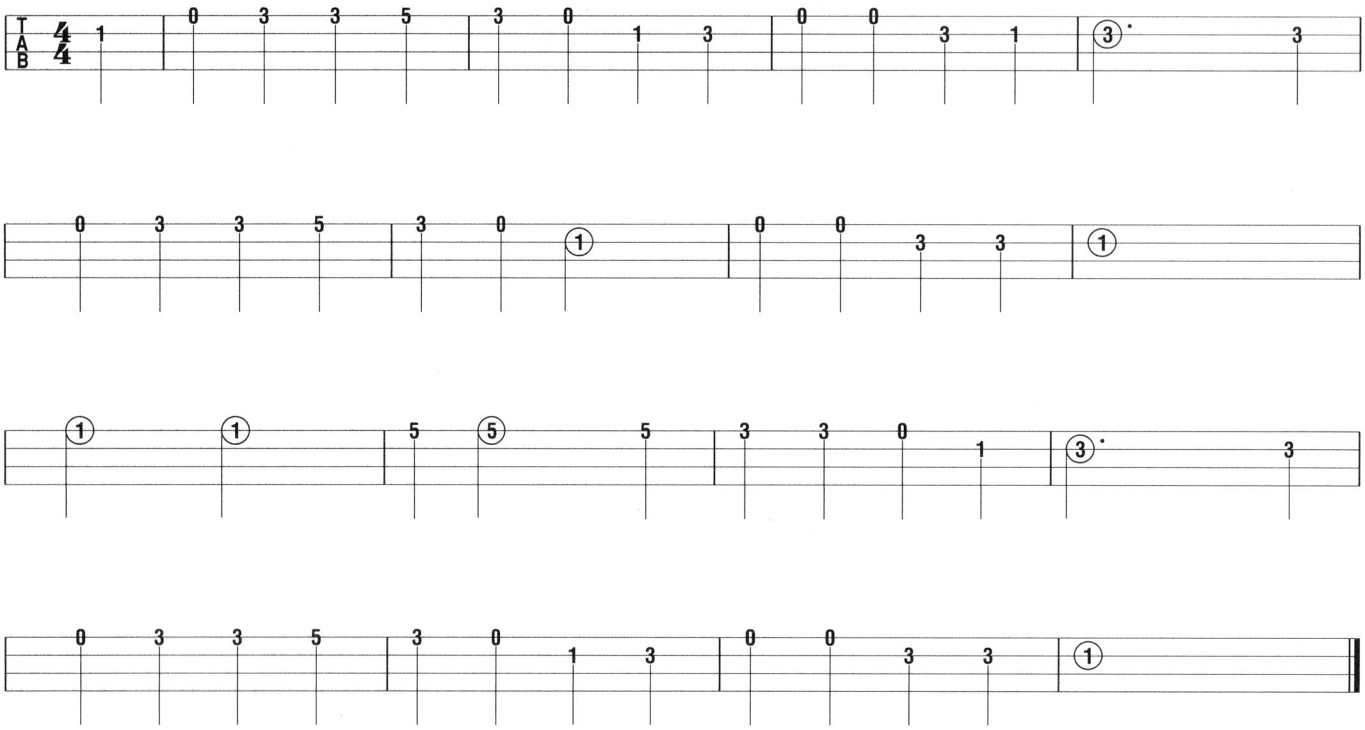

Dotted Half Notes

In the last song, did you notice the half notes with dots next to them? This type of note is called a *dotted half note*. Whenever a dot is attached to a note like this, we add half of the note's original value to that note's duration. So, since a half note is worth two beats, a dotted half note gets three beats.

Let's wrap up this chapter with a beautiful classical piece by Beethoven, "Ode to Joy."

Ode to Joy

from SYMPHONY NO. 9 IN D MINOR, FOURTH MOVEMENT CHORAL THEME
Words by Henry van Dyke
Music by Ludwig van Beethoven

CHAPTER 3

Adding the Third and Fourth Strings

Notes on the Third String

Let's expand our range on the instrument and learn some notes on the other strings, starting with the notes on string 3. On this string, we have an open C and a 2nd-fret D. Use finger 2 (middle) to fret the D note.

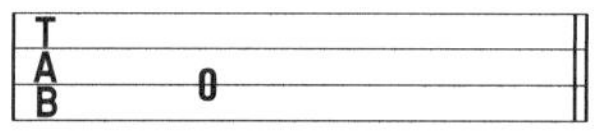

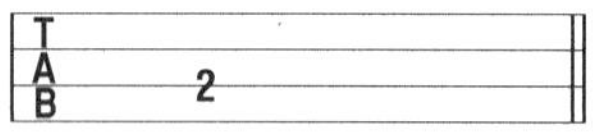

If you're confused about the fact that you already learned a C note and a D note on string 1, it's important to understand that the musical alphabet only uses the letters A through G, repeating the pattern over and over. So, the new notes you just learned are simply an *octave* below the notes using the same letters on string 1. Notes that are an octave apart are eight note names apart, which, when using the repeating A–G pattern, end up being the same letter.

Of course, C and D aren't the only notes we can play on the first few frets of string 3. The notes on the 1st and 3rd frets are sharps/flats. Remember, a sharp raises any note by one fret, while a flat lowers any note by one fret. So, the note found on the 1st fret on string 3 may be called either a C♯ or a D♭ because it lies one fret up from C and it lies one fret down from D. These two notes (C♯ and D♭) are basically the same note—they sound exactly the same and are played on the same fret—but we generally stick with one name or the other in the same song.

In general, we won't use string 4 much for melodies, as it's tuned higher than strings 2 and 3. Having the strings tuned out of order like this is called ***reentrant tuning*** *and is what gives the uke a unique sound when strummed; the strings on most other stringed instruments are tuned in order, low to high. We will include string 4 when strumming chords, but it will only occasionally provide an option for playing a note or two in a melody line.*

Let's try a familiar melody now, "Yankee Doodle," using our new notes.

Yankee Doodle

Traditional

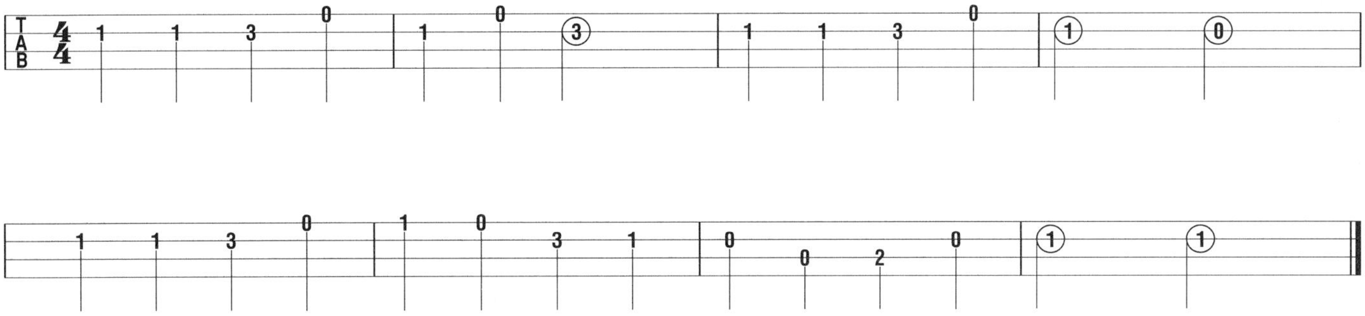

Ties

The next two songs include a musical symbol called a *tie*. A tie is a curved line connecting two notes of the same pitch, and it simply adds the values of the two notes together, making one longer note. You only pluck the first note included in the tie, adding the time value of the second note to the duration of the first note. In the system of notation used in this book, the tab number and notehead will not be repeated for the second note; simply keep holding down the same note when you see this. For the pick-up notes in "When the Saints Go Marching In," count "one" and then play the first three notes on counts two, three, and four of the pick-up measure.

When the Saints Go Marching In

Traditional

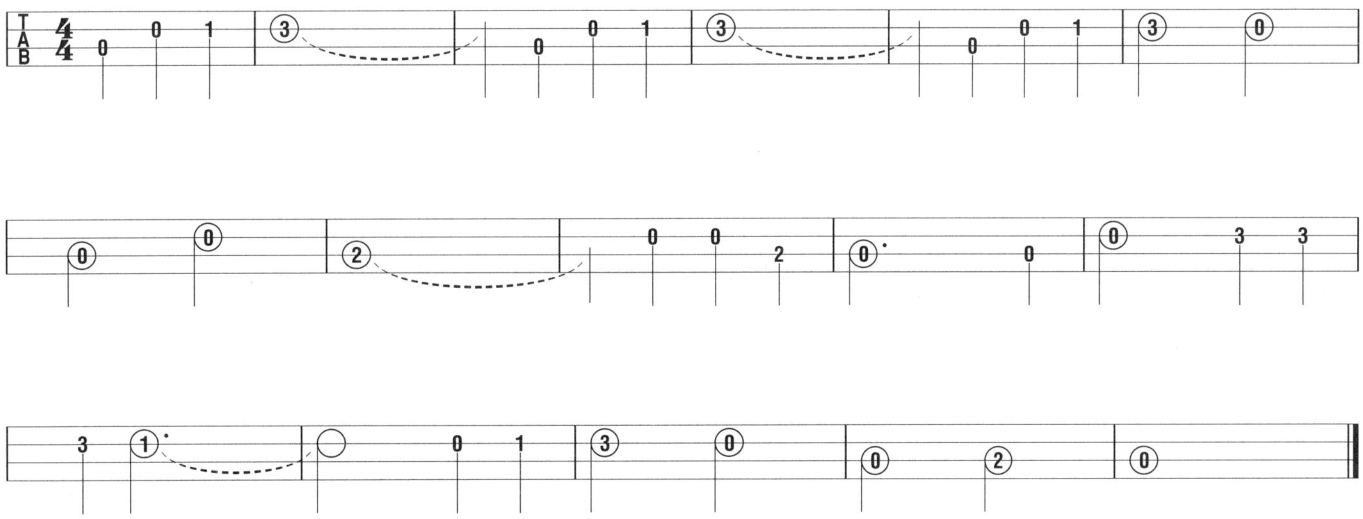

3/4 Time Signature

Instead of having four beats in a measure like we saw in our previous songs, some songs will have three beats in each measure. When this is the case, you'll see a *3/4 time signature* instead of a 4/4 time signature at the start. The quarter note will still receive the beat, but you'll only count up to three, not four, in each measure.

Our next song, "Amazing Grace," is in *3/4 time* and includes one pick-up note. Always remember to look out for pick-up notes and check the time signature of a song before you start playing, and adjust your counting accordingly.

Amazing Grace

Words by John Newton
Traditional American Melody

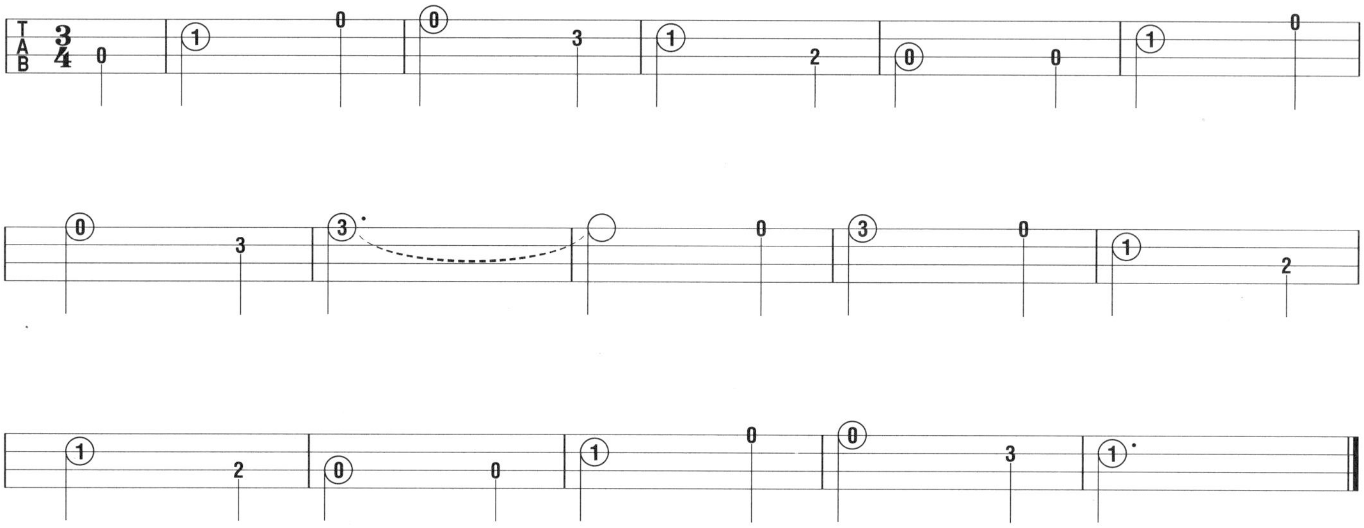

Eighth Notes

An *eighth note* gets one half beat, meaning two eighth notes equal one quarter note. If you count "**one**-and, **two**-and, **three**-and, **four**-and," each syllable represents one eighth note. A single eighth note looks like a quarter note with a small "flag" attached, and consecutive eighth notes are connected with a beam. In "Frère Jacques," four consecutive eighth notes are used at the beginning of measures 5 and 6.

Frère Jacques (Are You Sleeping?)

Traditional

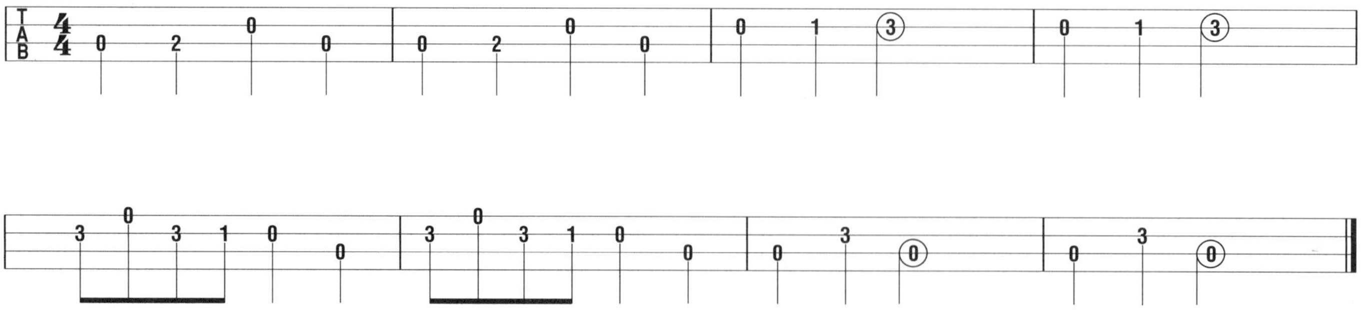

In "Happy Birthday," the eighth notes come in groupings of two, still connected by a beam. Notice that this one is in 3/4, and the first two eighth notes are played over the final beat of the pick-up measure (on beat three and beat "three-and").

Happy Birthday

Words and Music by Mildred J. Hill and Patty S. Hill

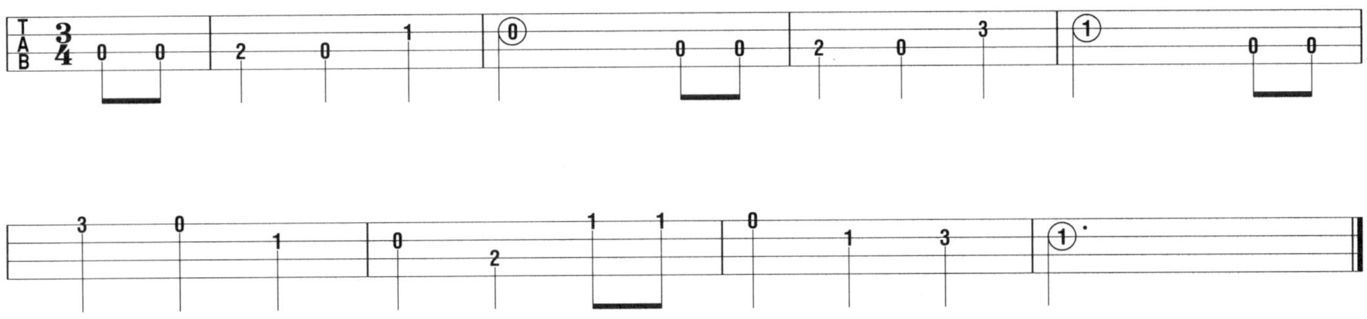

We'll finish this chapter up with a standard blues melody that is almost entirely made up of eighth notes, plus we'll preview a few new notes for fun. To fret the note on the 4th fret of string 3, use finger 4 (pinky). For the notes on the 5th and 6th fret of string 1, you can either use the pinky for both (although repeating a finger like this is a habit you don't want to get into) or you can move your hand out of position briefly to play the 5th fret with finger 1 and the 6th fret with finger 2, moving back to your original hand position to play the 3rd fret with finger 3.

"Standard Blues Melody"

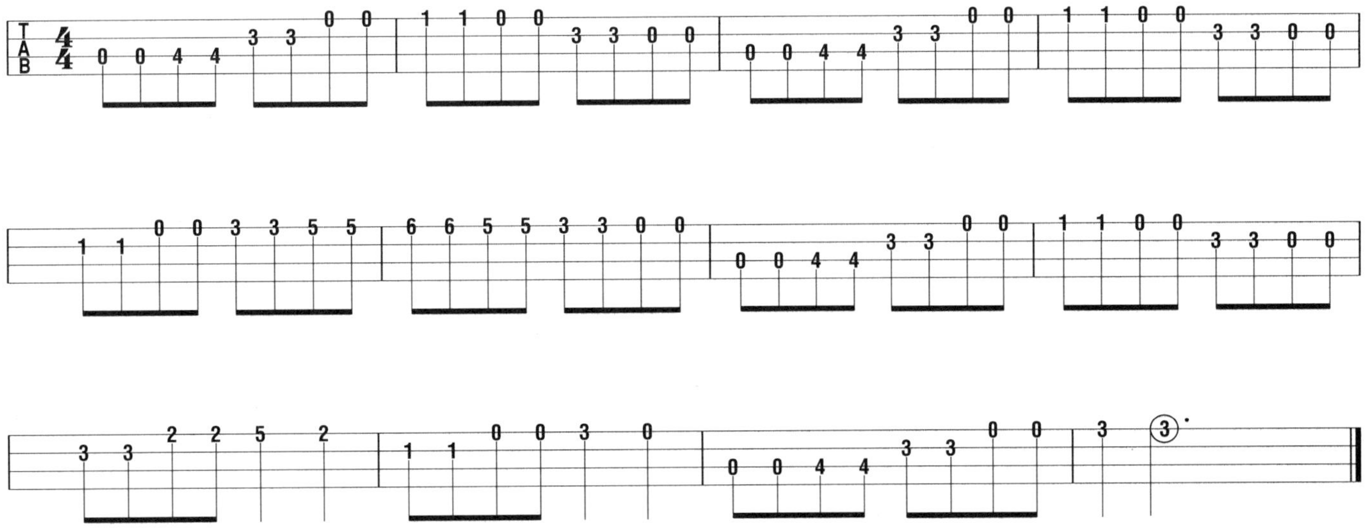

CHAPTER 4

Chords and Basic Strumming

When we play three or more notes together, we're playing a *chord*. Playing chords on the ukulele is very popular, as many players enjoy strumming chords while singing along. It's particularly important when playing chords to fret the notes with the tips of your fingers, because otherwise you might accidentally mute a string that should be ringing out.

Reading Chord Diagrams

Chord diagrams are used to show you where to put your fingers on the fretboard to play chords. Think of a chord diagram as a map or picture of your ukulele's fretboard, with the head of the uke pointing up and the fretboard facing you. The dots show which strings and frets to place your fingers on, while the numbers show which fingers to use. An "O" behind the nut indicates that the string isn't fretted but instead is played "open." (Conversely, if you see an "X" above the nut, it means that the string isn't played at all.)

For the following C chord, use finger 3 on the 3rd fret of string 1. Then strum all four strings with your right-hand thumb in a downward motion. For clarity, we'll also include the tab for the chords throughout this book.

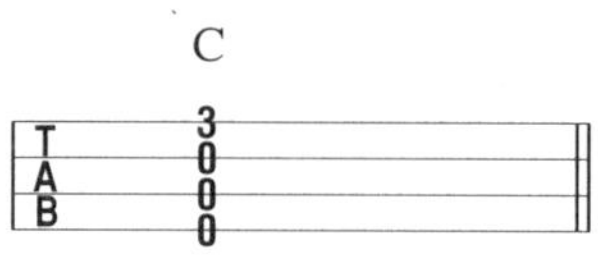

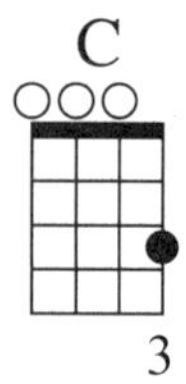

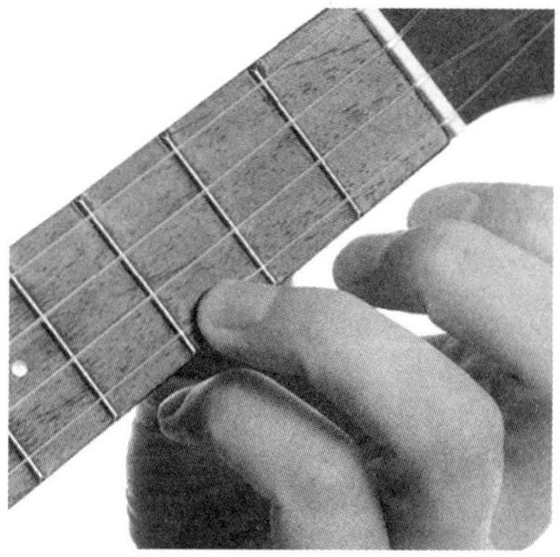

Now let's try an F chord. For this chord, place finger 2 on the 2nd fret of string 4, and finger 1 on the 1st fret of string 2. Again, strum all four strings, making sure that the open strings (3 and 1) are clearly ringing. Play each string individually while holding down the chord to verify nothing is muted. Remember to use your fingertips! (**Note:** The hand demonstrating the chords/notes in many of these photos is held in a way to show the fretboard and fingerings clearly, but you should actually keep your unused fingers relaxed; don't hold unneeded tension in your hand or force your fingers off to the side of the fretboard as you'll sometimes see in the photos.)

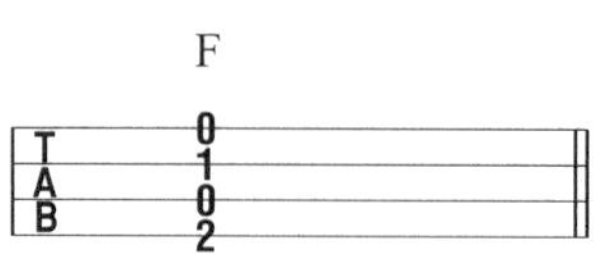

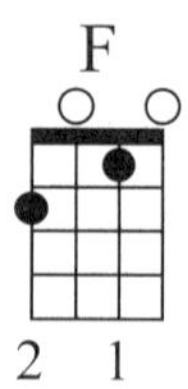

Practice changing between all new chords that you learn. When moving from one chord to another, it's normal to have to pause a bit between them at first, but with practice you'll be able to move between the chords quickly.

Let's try switching between the C and F chords in a song. We'll be strumming a quarter-note rhythm, as shown in the music. Watch the chord symbols above the music to determine when to change chords. When you feel comfortable with the strumming, try singing along!

Imagine

Words and Music by John Lennon

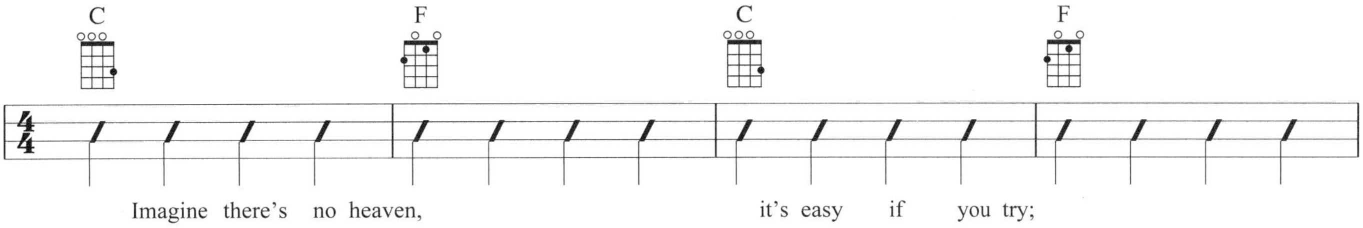

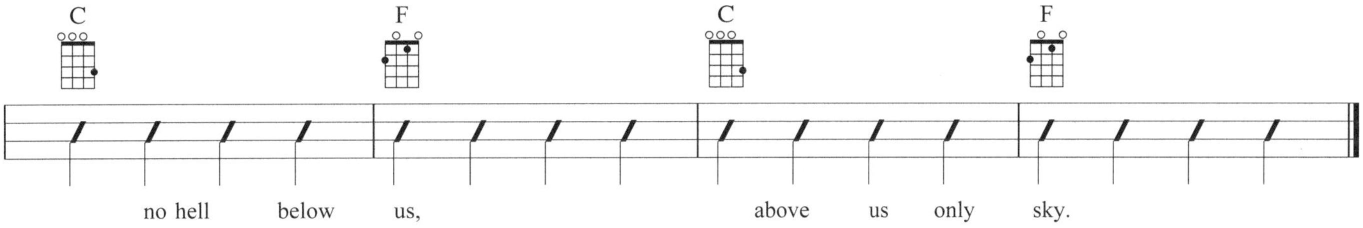

Now let's learn the G chord. This one will require using three fingers, so it will take some practice to be able to grab the chord quickly. Place finger 1 on the 2nd fret of string 3; use finger 3 on the 3rd fret of string 2; and finally, employ finger 2 on the 2nd fret of string 1. String 4 will be played open.

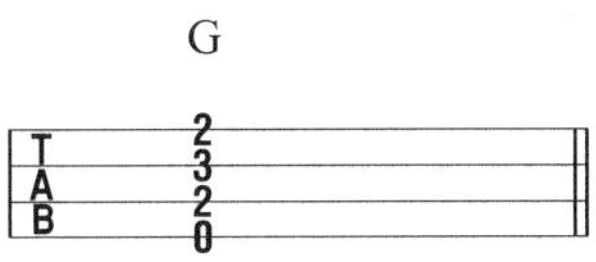

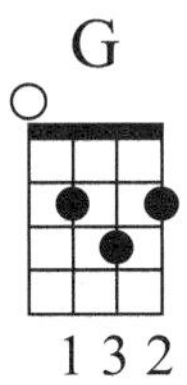

Let's put that G chord to work in a new song. In this case, the vocal melody line includes three pick-up notes, so start strumming after you sing the first three words. (**Note:** The symbols above the first three words in the tab are called *rests* and indicate that nothing should be played.)

You Are My Sunshine

Words and Music by Jimmie Davis

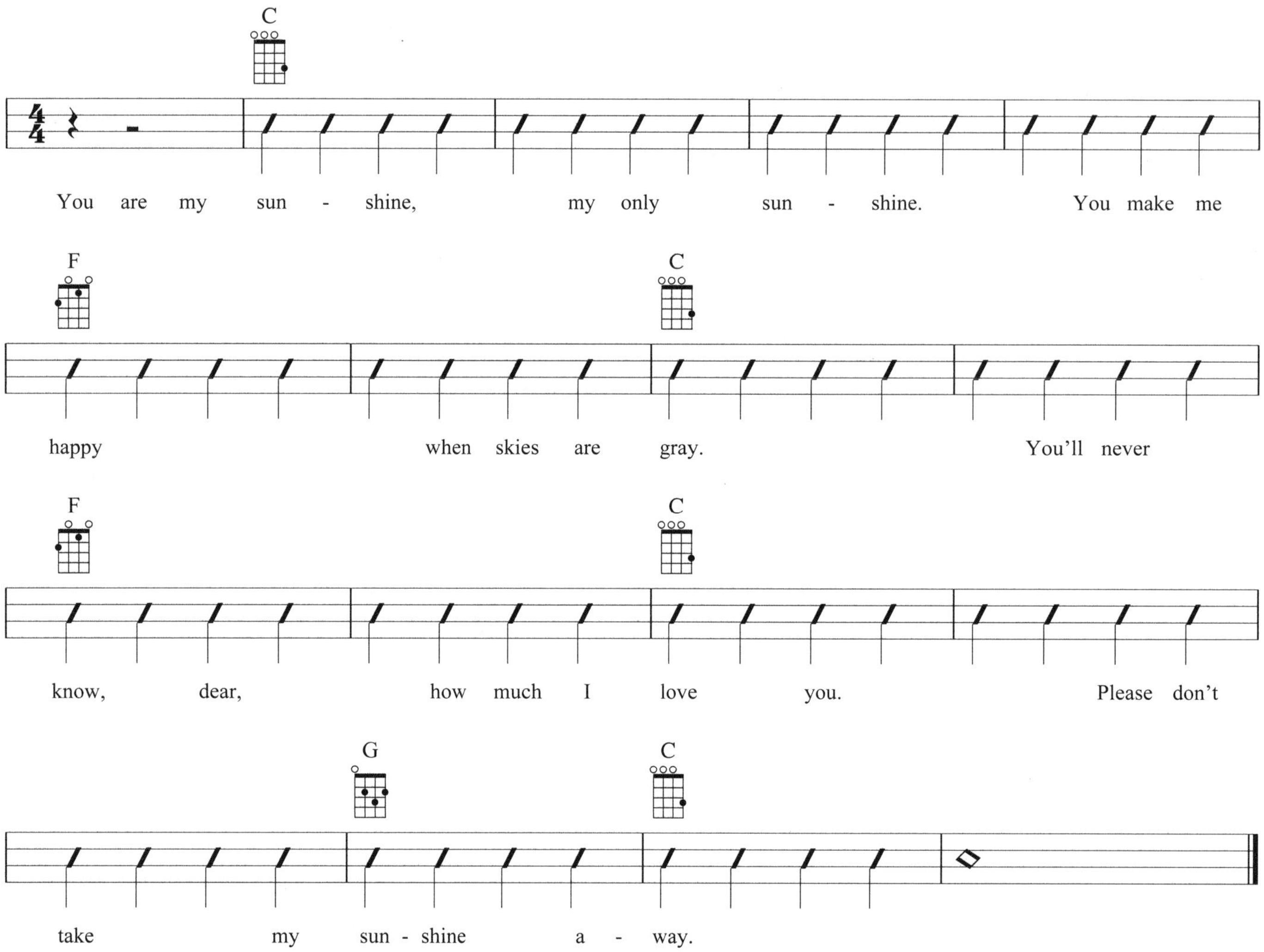

Do your best to make your chord changes in time. Strive to visualize the next chord and prepare your fingers. Instead of putting one finger down at a time to fret a chord, try to arrange the fingers in the air, first, and then pop them down as a unit. If you're having trouble, just spend some time repeatedly changing from chord to chord. Simply take two chords and strum once for each one. Everyone struggles with this at first, so be patient—you'll get it!

Here's another great song using the three chords we know. This song has a faster tempo, so we'll just strum two half notes in each measure.

Down on the Corner

Words and Music by John Fogerty

We can take the G chord we already know and just change one note to get a G7 chord. So, now we'll play string 3 on the 2nd fret with finger 2; string 2 on the 1st fret with finger 1; and string 1 on the 2nd fret with finger 3.

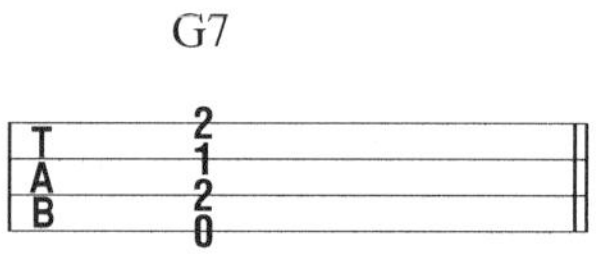

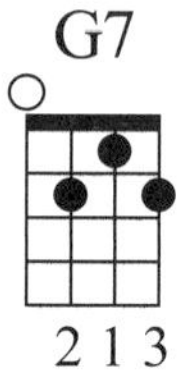

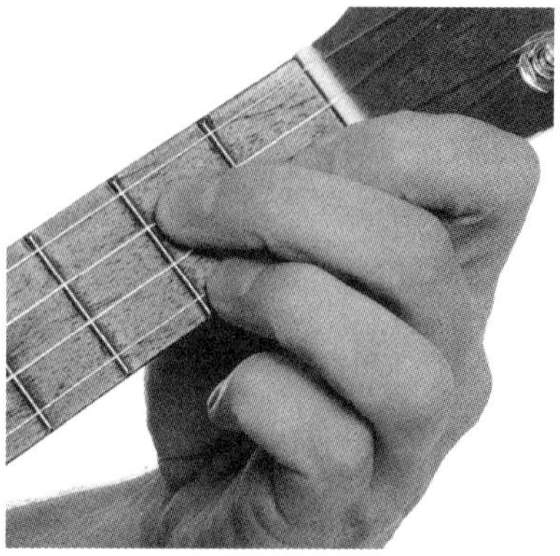

Try out the G7 chord in the chorus of this popular Beatles tune.

Hey Jude

Words and Music by John Lennon and Paul McCartney

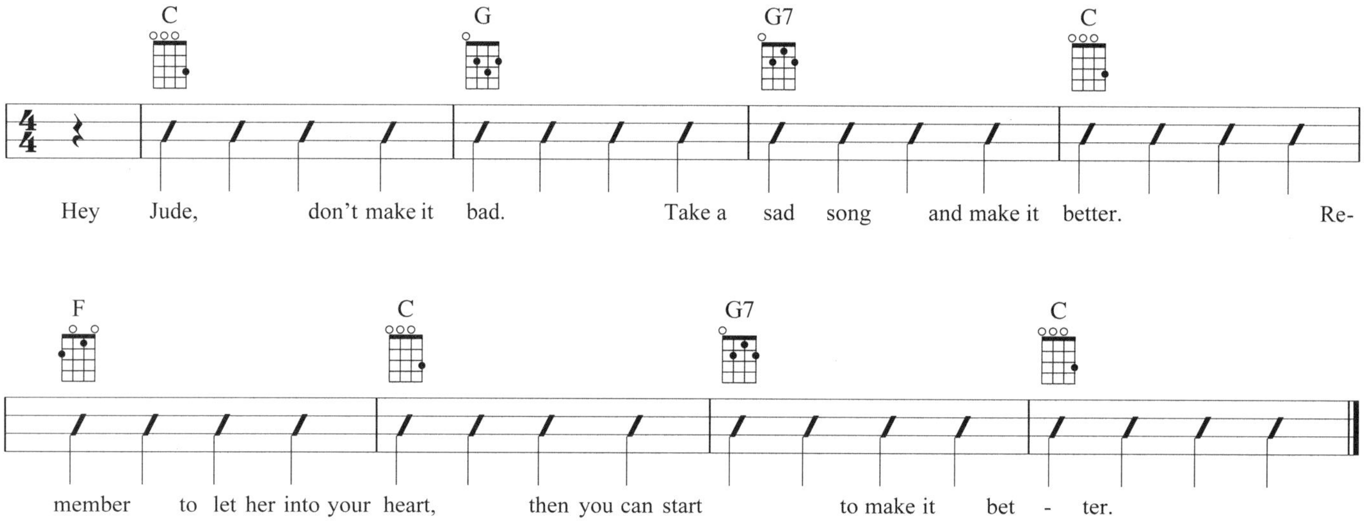

Let's add another chord to our repertoire: Am (pronounced "A-minor"). To play the Am chord, simply put finger 2 on the 2nd fret of string 4. That's it! The other three strings are played open. This chord is like an F chord without finger 1.

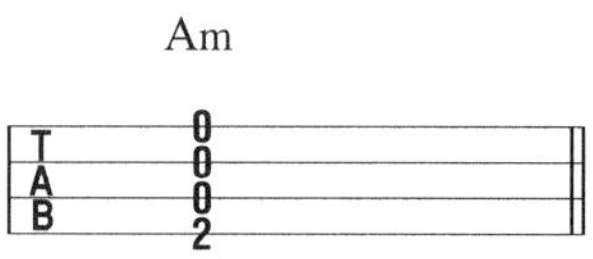

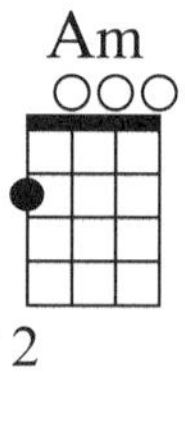

We can use the Am chord in the chorus of this hit song by Adele.

Someone Like You

Words and Music by Adele Adkins and Dan Wilson

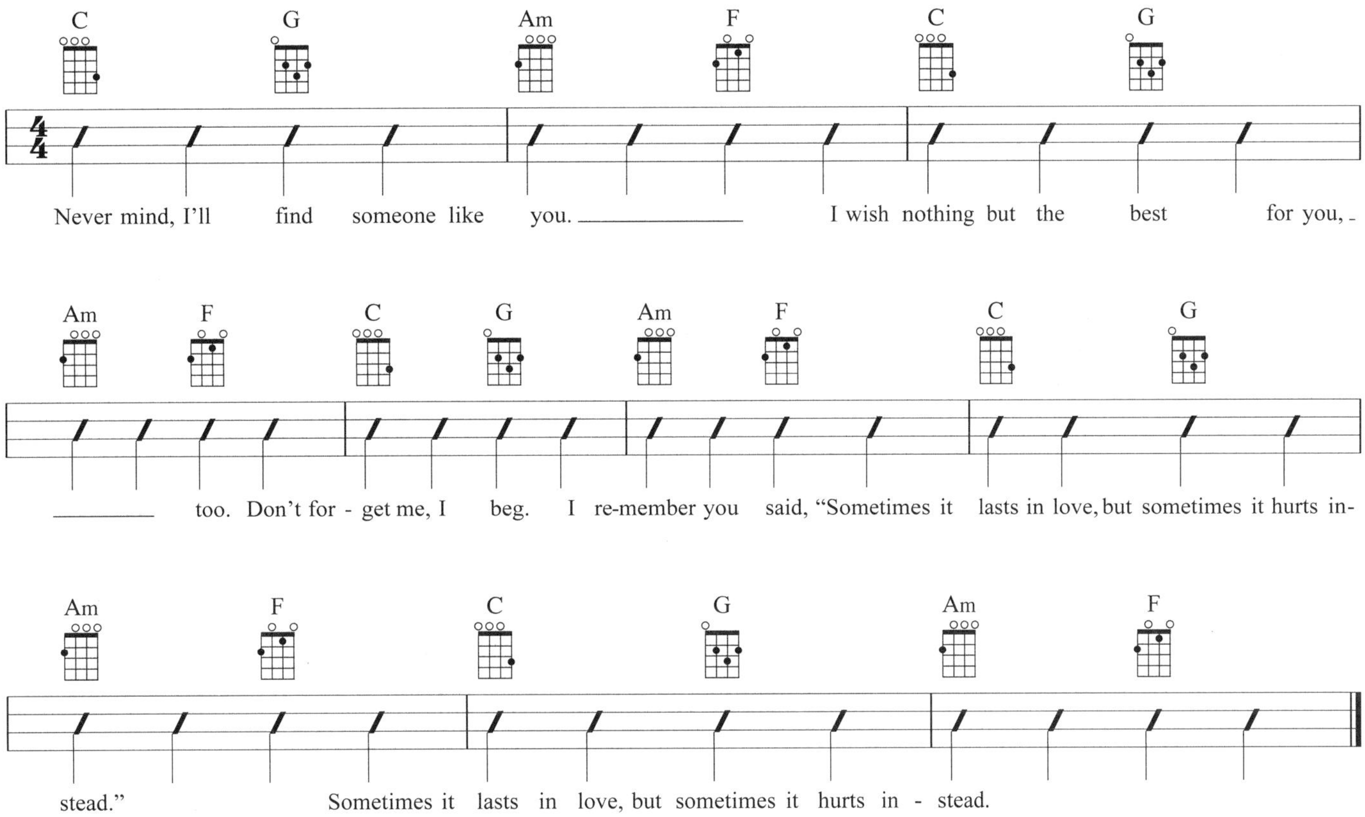

Repeat Signs

Repeat signs 𝄆 𝄇 are used to enclose a section that should be played once again. When you see two repeat signs in a piece of music—a backwards-facing one and a forward-facing one—simply go back to the forward-facing repeat sign as soon as you hit the backwards-facing one, repeating the section enclosed by the repeat signs just once. Sometimes in printed music you'll see only one backwards-facing repeat sign. In this case, simply go back to the beginning of the piece and play through the section again. Unless otherwise marked, you'll only repeat a section once, ignoring the repeat sign the second time around if there is more music to be played beyond it.

First and Second Endings

When we repeat a part but want that part to end a little differently the second time through, we use separate endings so that we don't have to write out the entire part all over again. We call these *first endings* and *second endings*. Numbered brackets above the tab are used to show the different endings, and repeat signs are used to help navigate through the endings.

Let's look at how to use the first and second endings in the next song. When you reach the forward-facing repeat sign, ignore it, but note where it is. When you reach the backwards-facing repeat sign at the end of the first ending, go back to the forward-facing repeat sign and play through the verse and chorus again—and if you're singing along, sing the second line of lyrics. Then, the second time through, skip the first ending and close out the piece with the second ending.

Let It Be

Words and Music by John Lennon and Paul McCartney

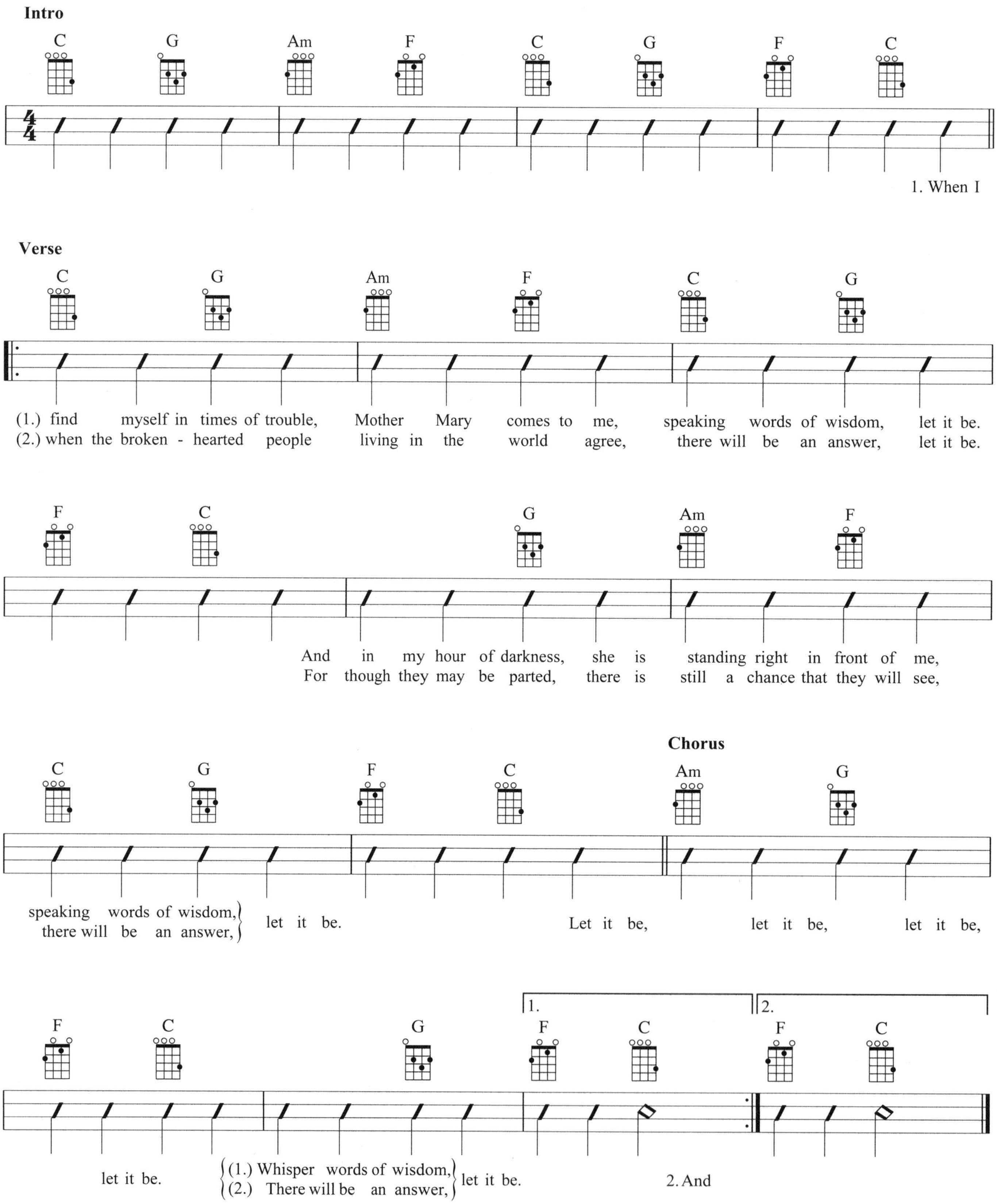

CHAPTER 5

More Chords and New Strumming Patterns

While you'll find that there are countless songs you can play with just the five chords you've learned so far, it's best to become familiar with many chords to help expand your repertoire. Having already learned some chords, you can see that it's just a matter of getting familiar with the new fingerings and memorizing the chord shapes. In this chapter, we'll learn a few more chords in a progressive manner, and we'll also take a look at a few different strumming patterns.

First, let's take a look at the A and D chords.

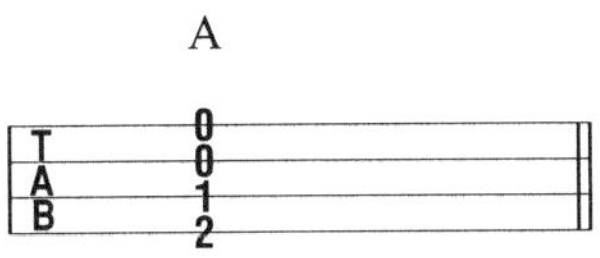

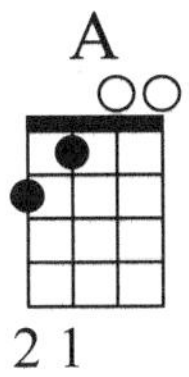

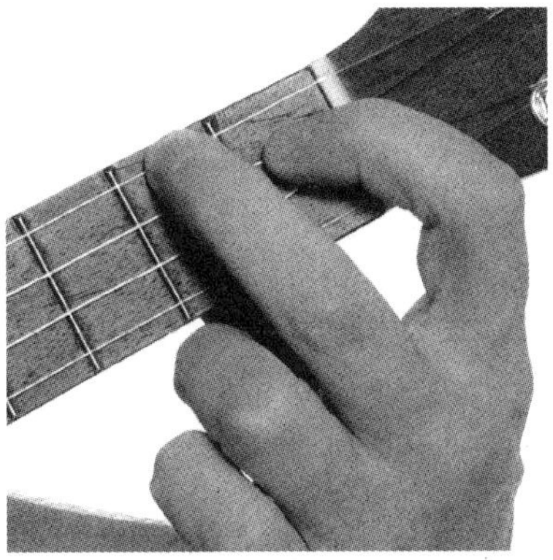

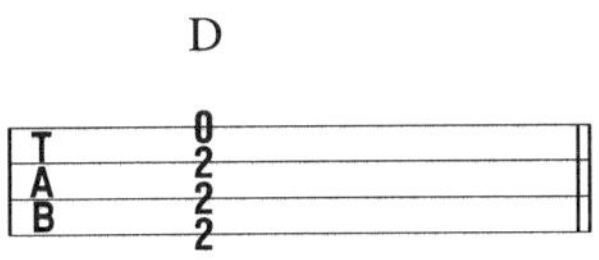

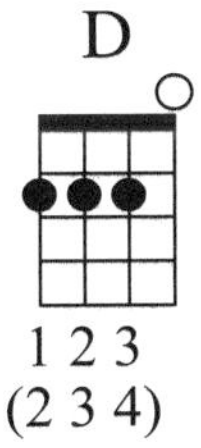

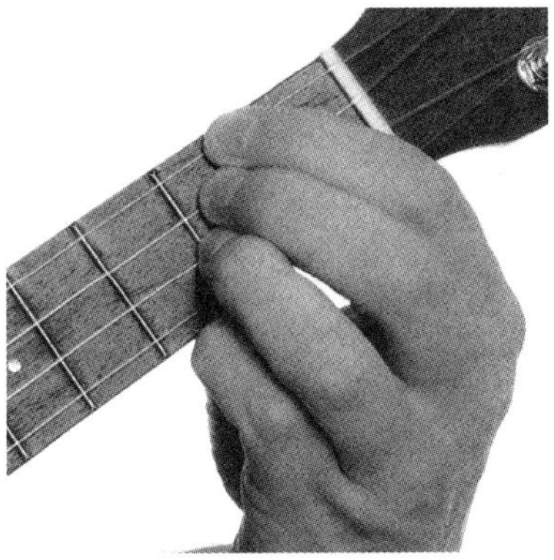

It can be tricky to cram those three fingers used for the D chord all on one fret, so make sure you're using your fingertips. Notice that two different fingerings are shown under the chord diagram for the D chord. The 1-2-3 fingering (as shown in the photo) is a common way to grab this chord; however, the 2-3-4 fingering will allow you to leave finger 2 down on the 2nd fret of string 4 when switching between the A and D chords.

As you continue with your ukulele journey, you'll encounter songs using chords that you don't know. Instead of passing on learning these songs, use them as an opportunity to expand your chord knowledge. Every new chord will seem a bit awkward and difficult at first, but give it time and soon enough any new chord will feel comfortable!

Strumming Patterns Using Eighth Notes

Remember in chapter 3 when we learned eighth notes? Let's put those eighth notes to work in a few new strumming patterns. Up to this point, we've just been strumming quarter notes using *downstrokes*. When we strum eighth notes, we add an *upstroke* to the mix, strumming the strings in an upward fashion from the floor to the ceiling. If you're not using a pick to strum, the easiest way to do this will be to use your index finger on your right hand for both the downstroke and the upstroke. But for the more traditional ukulele strumming sound, try using your thumb on the downstrokes and your index finger on the upstrokes.

For practice, here's a new strumming pattern that includes eighth notes. The downstrokes are indicated with this symbol: ⊓. The upstrokes are identified with a different symbol: V. Repeat this short exercise on the A chord until it feels natural (and feel free to try the strumming pattern with other chords).

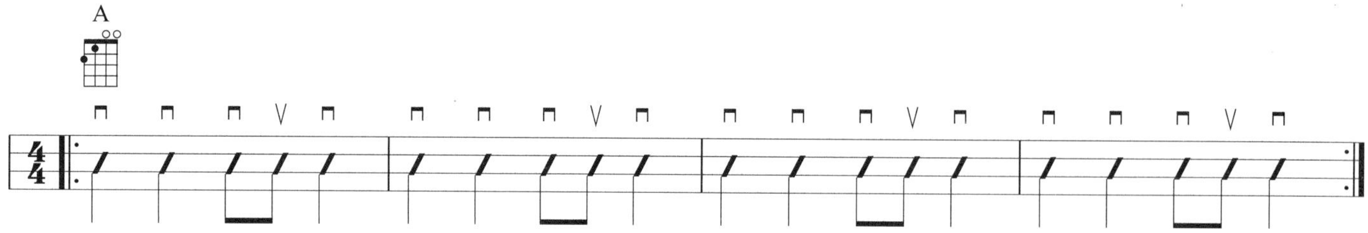

Let's try our new strumming pattern in a well-known Bob Marley song.

Three Little Birds

Words and Music by Bob Marley

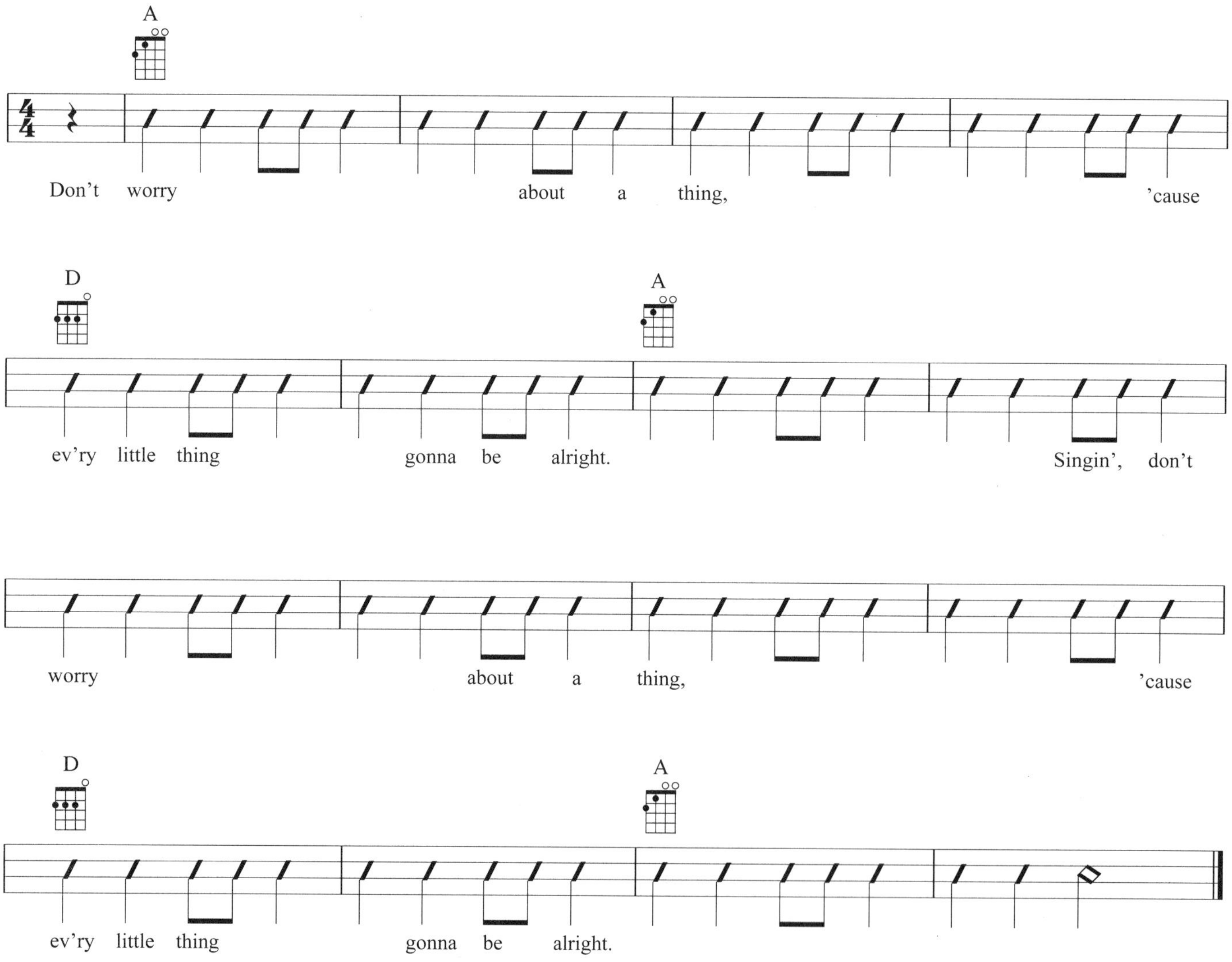

This next chord, Em (pronounced "E minor"), is definitely the hardest chord we've learned yet. At first, you'll most likely need to put down one finger at a time, but again, it will be better in the long run if you're able to "form the chord in the air" and place all fingers down together. Be patient... this takes time! (**Note:** If you'd like to start with an easier three-finger Em chord, it's OK to leave string 4 open and use finger 3, not finger 4, on string 3.)

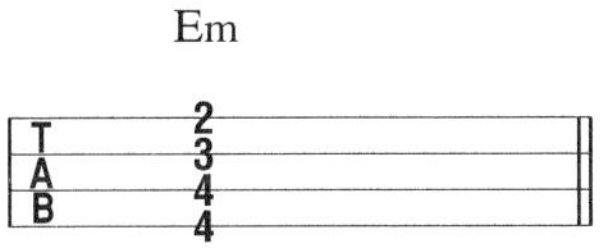

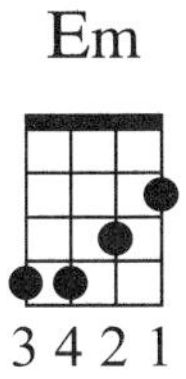

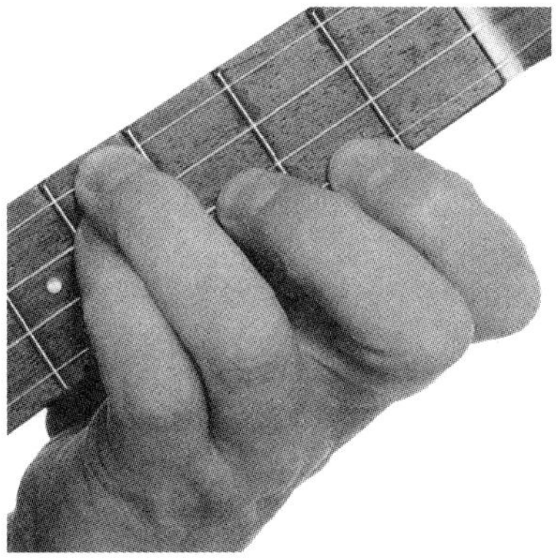

"Good Riddance (Time of Your Life)," uses the Em chord as well as the G, C, and D chords. (As a goal, try to memorize all new chords as you learn them.) We also have a new strumming pattern that includes a few tied eighth notes. Just like ties can connect single notes, they can also be used in a strumming pattern to connect chords across beats. In this case, beat "two-and" and beat three are tied, and the tricky part will be to play the two consecutive upstrokes on beat "two-and" and beat "three-and" while playing nothing on beat three. To do this, you need to essentially "miss" the strings on beat three with a downstroke motion, keeping the hand moving to prepare the upstroke. (**Note:** Whenever you see that the downstroke and upstroke indicators have disappeared from above a piece of music, simply continue using the same pattern.)

Good Riddance (Time of Your Life)

Words by Billie Joe
Music by Green Day

Intro

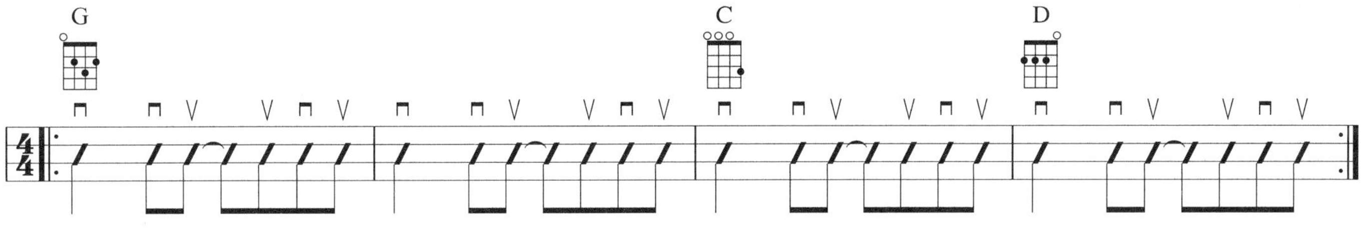

Verse

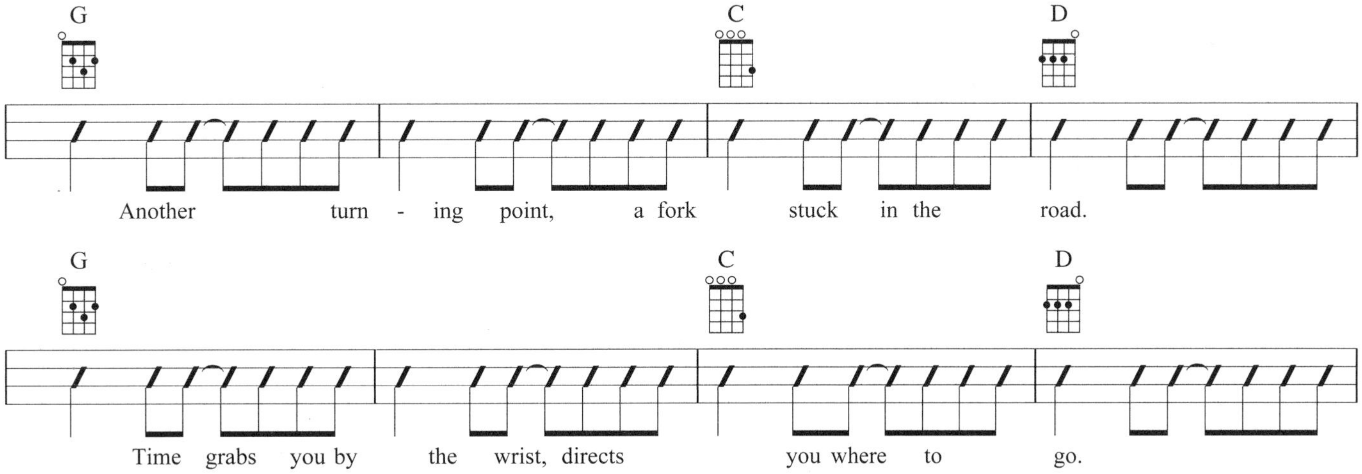

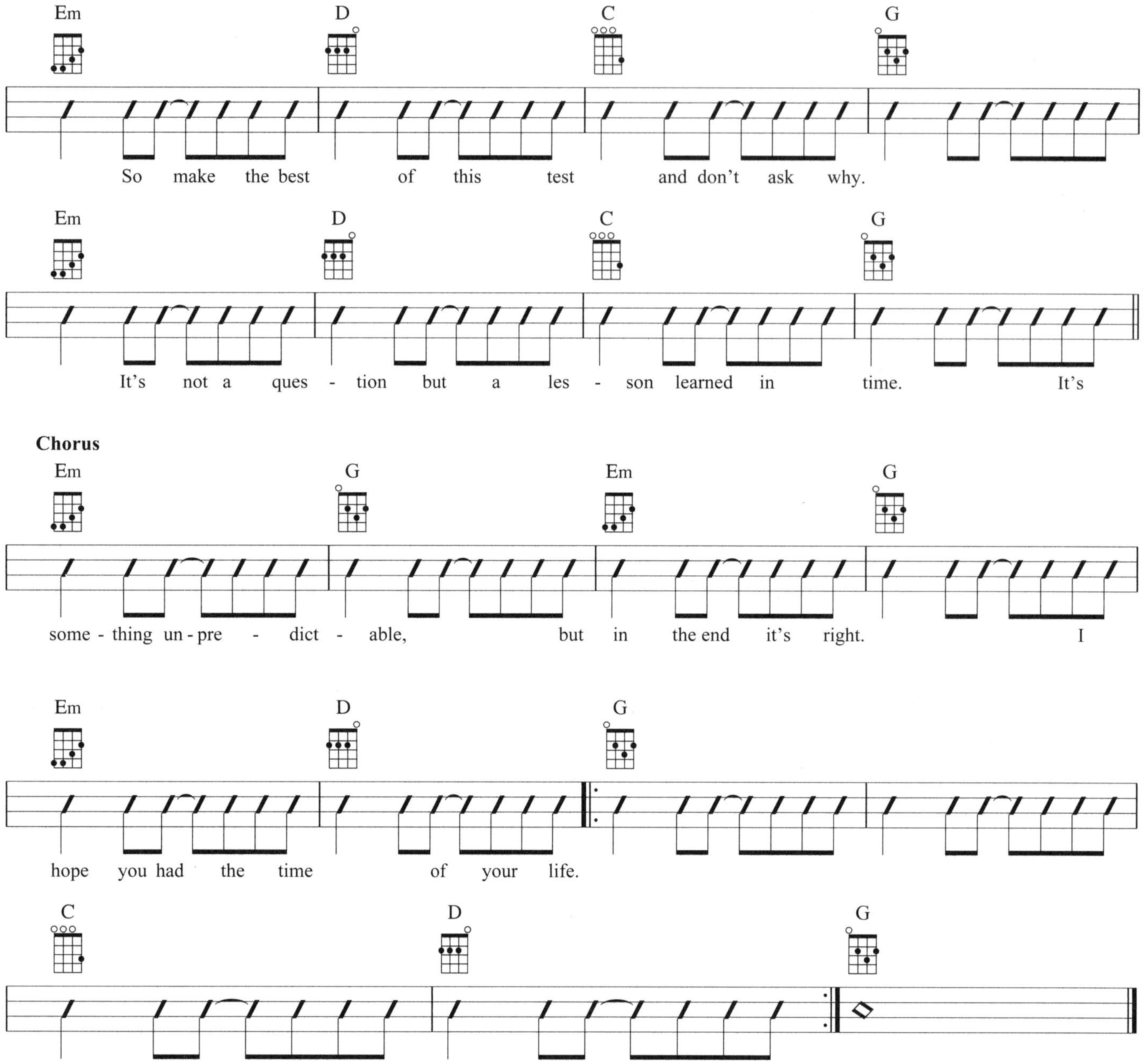

Again, if singing and playing at the same time is proving to be quite the challenge, just concentrate on the ukulele part for a while. Once you get more comfortable with the uke, you'll be able to sing along. Keep trying but don't get discouraged. It can be difficult!

Let's learn two more chords, F♯m (pronounced "F-sharp minor") and E7, and then put them to use in the classic hit "Stand by Me."

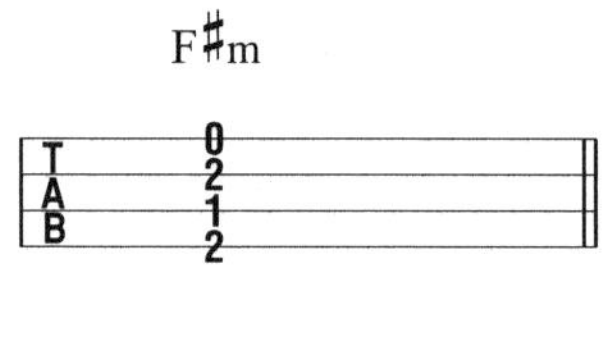

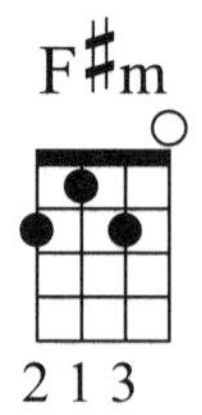

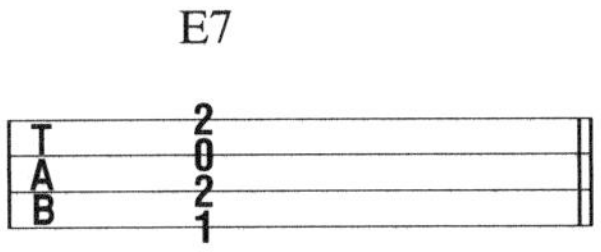

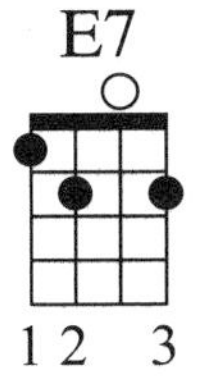

In "Stand by Me," we'll use a strumming pattern with tied notes, but this time the rhythm will be a bit different. Here, you'll be "missing" the strings on beat "one-and" and beat "two-and" (for the quarter notes) plus beat three (for the eighth note that's tied to the strum before it) but you'll strum the strings with every other downstroke and upstroke.

Stand by Me

Words and Music by Jerry Leiber, Mike Stoller and Ben E. King

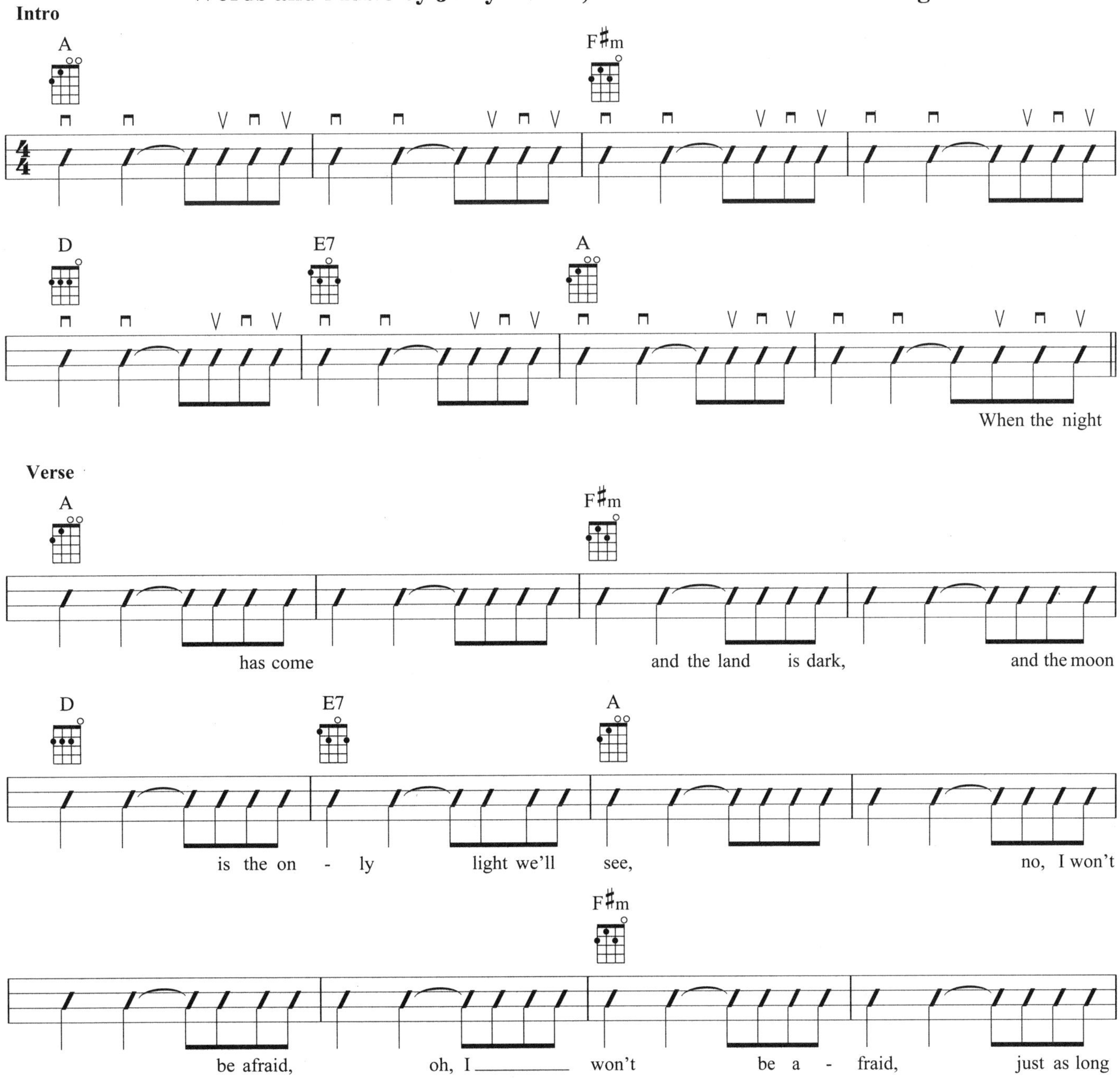

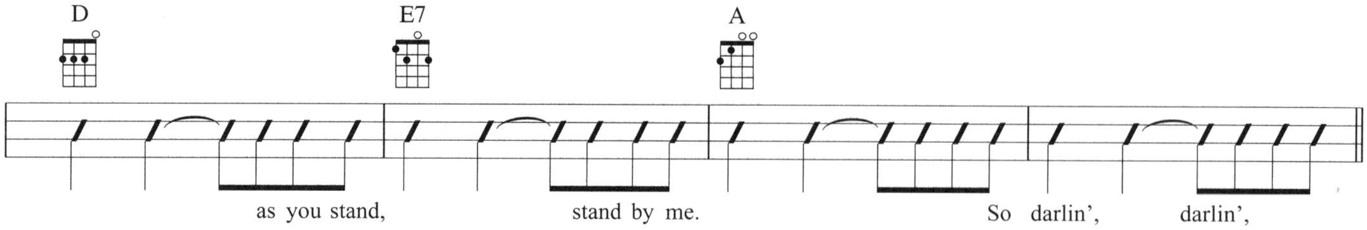

Chorus

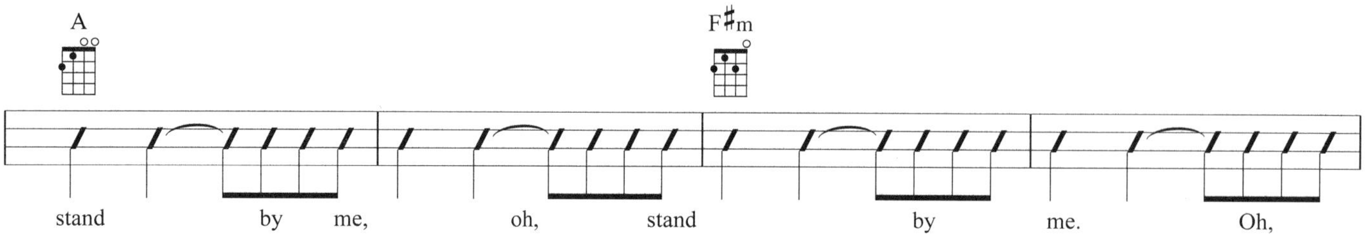

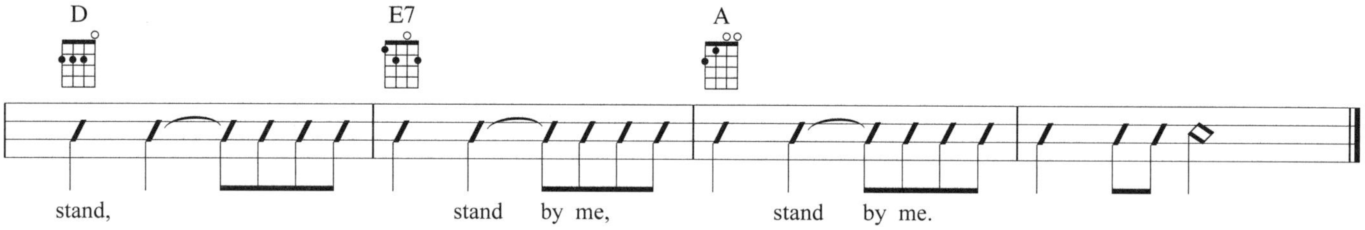

It's not uncommon for players to use more than one strumming pattern in the same song, so let's take the patterns we learned in "Good Riddance (Time of Your Life)" and "Stand by Me" and use them both in the next arrangement. We'll start with the "Stand by Me" pattern, but when we get to the chorus, we'll change to the other strumming pattern. "Riptide" uses some chords we learned early on, so it will also make for a good review. Remember, it's always important to look back and go over material you previously learned. You don't want to forget anything!

Riptide

Words and Music by Vance Joy

Intro

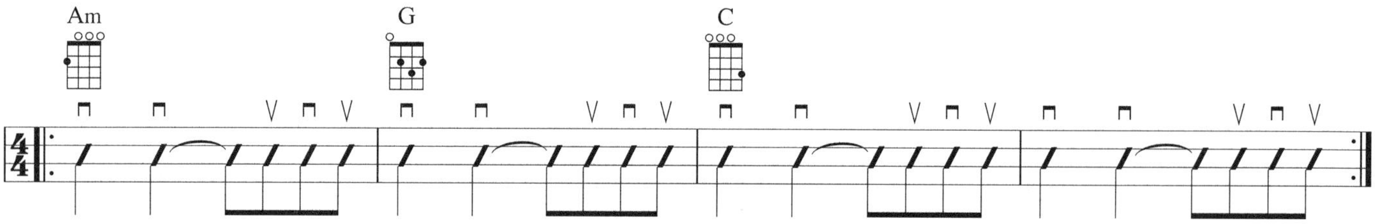

Verse

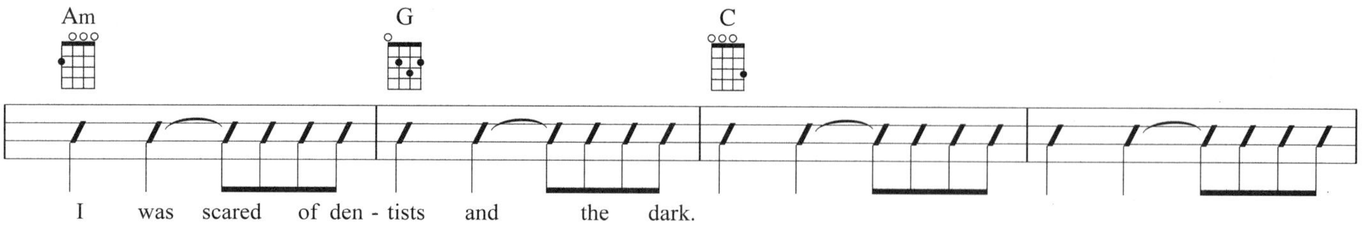

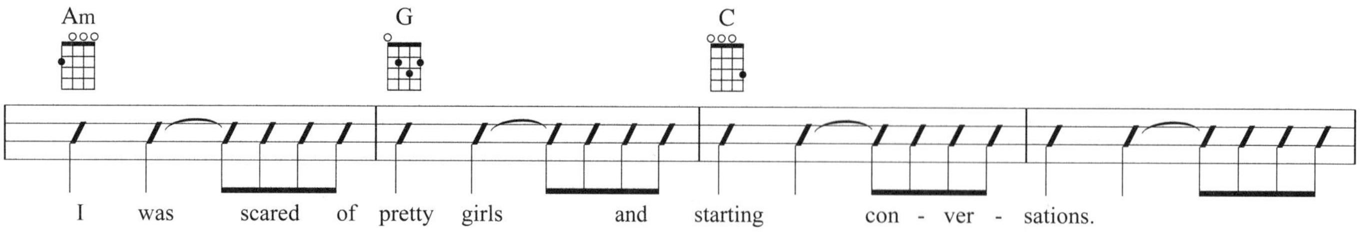

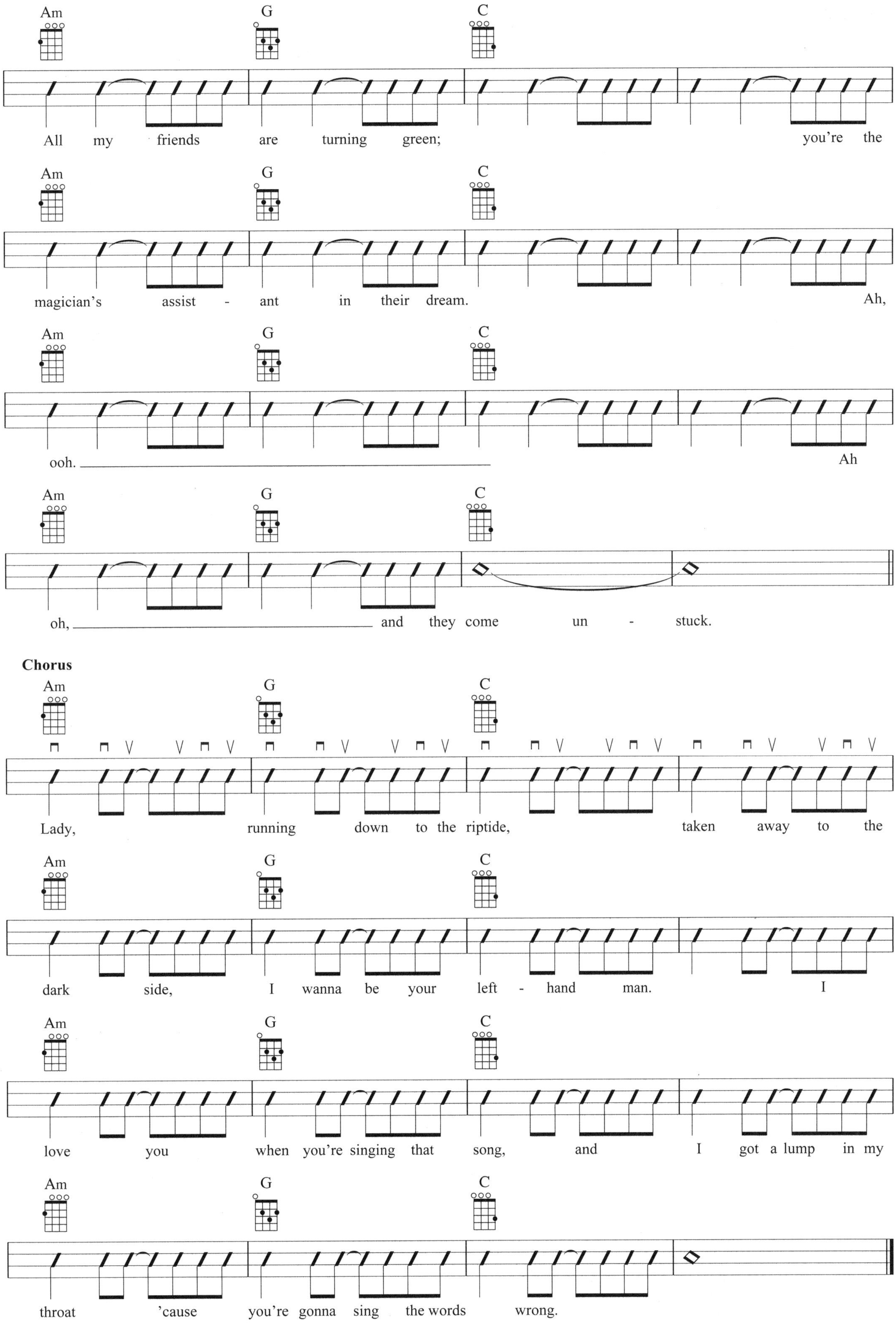
Am G C
All my friends are turning green; you're the
Am G C
magician's assist - ant in their dream. Ah,
Am G C
ooh. Ah
Am G C
oh, and they come un - stuck.
Chorus
Am G C
Lady, running down to the riptide, taken away to the
Am G C
dark side, I wanna be your left - hand man. I
Am G C
love you when you're singing that song, and I got a lump in my
Am G C
throat 'cause you're gonna sing the words wrong.

We'll conclude this chapter with the iconic ukulele hit "Over the Rainbow," arranged and performed by Israel "IZ" Kamakawiwo'ole. The new strumming pattern is just a slight variation of the "Good Riddance" pattern. The only difference here is that you'll also "miss" the strings with your upstroke on beat "four-and."

Over the Rainbow

from THE WIZARD OF OZ
Music by Harold Arlen
Lyric by E.Y. "Yip" Harburg

Verse

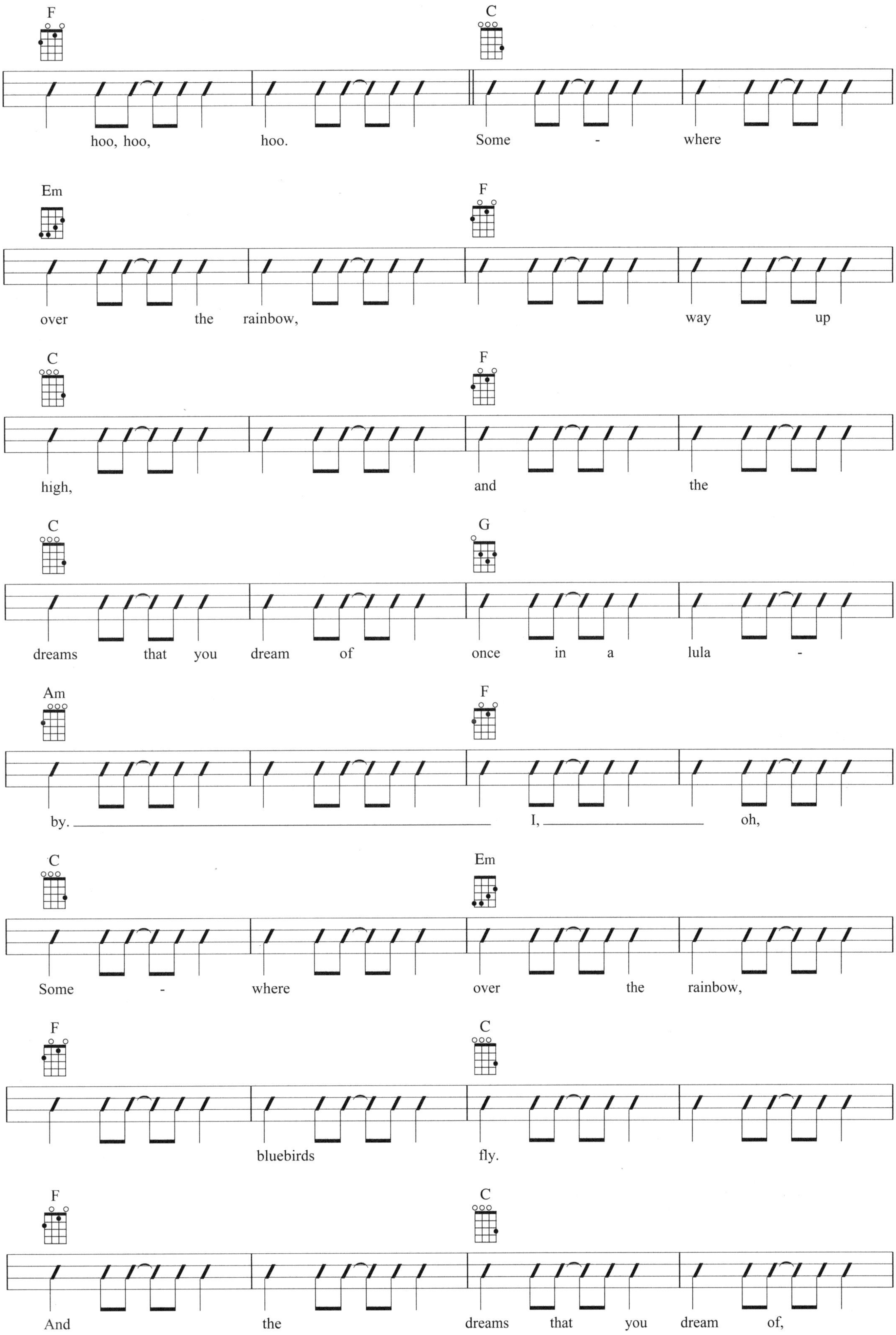
F C
hoo, hoo, hoo. Some - where
Em F
over the rainbow, way up
C F
high, and the
C G
dreams that you dream of once in a lula -
Am F
by. I, oh,
C Em
Some - where over the rainbow,
F C
bluebirds fly.
F C
And the dreams that you dream of,

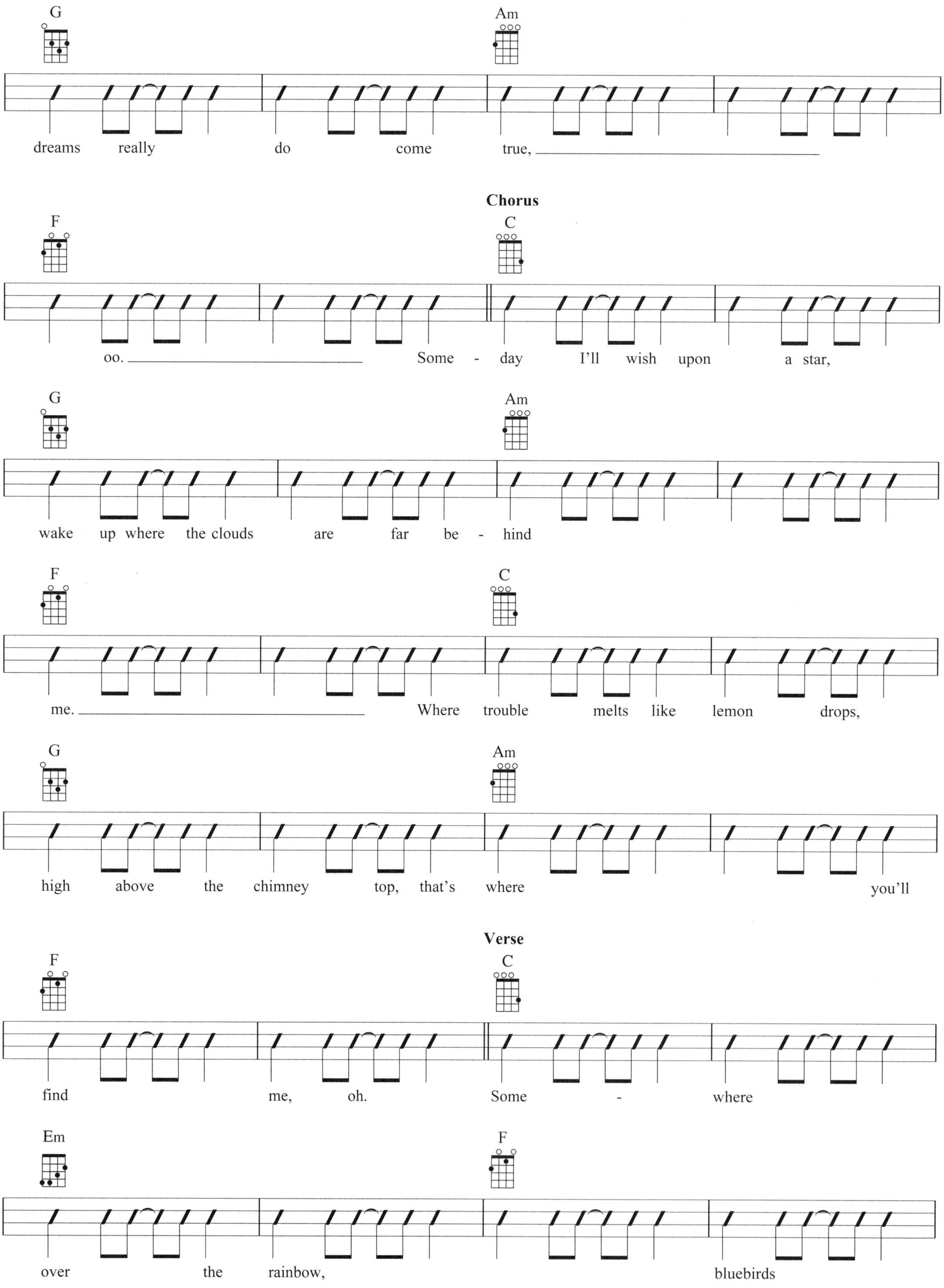
G
Am
dreams really do come true,
oo.
Chorus
F
C
Some - day I'll wish upon a star,
G
Am
wake up where the clouds are far be - hind
F
C
me.
Where trouble melts like lemon drops,
G
Am
high above the chimney top, that's where you'll
Verse
F
C
find me, oh.
Some - where
Em
F
over the rainbow,
bluebirds

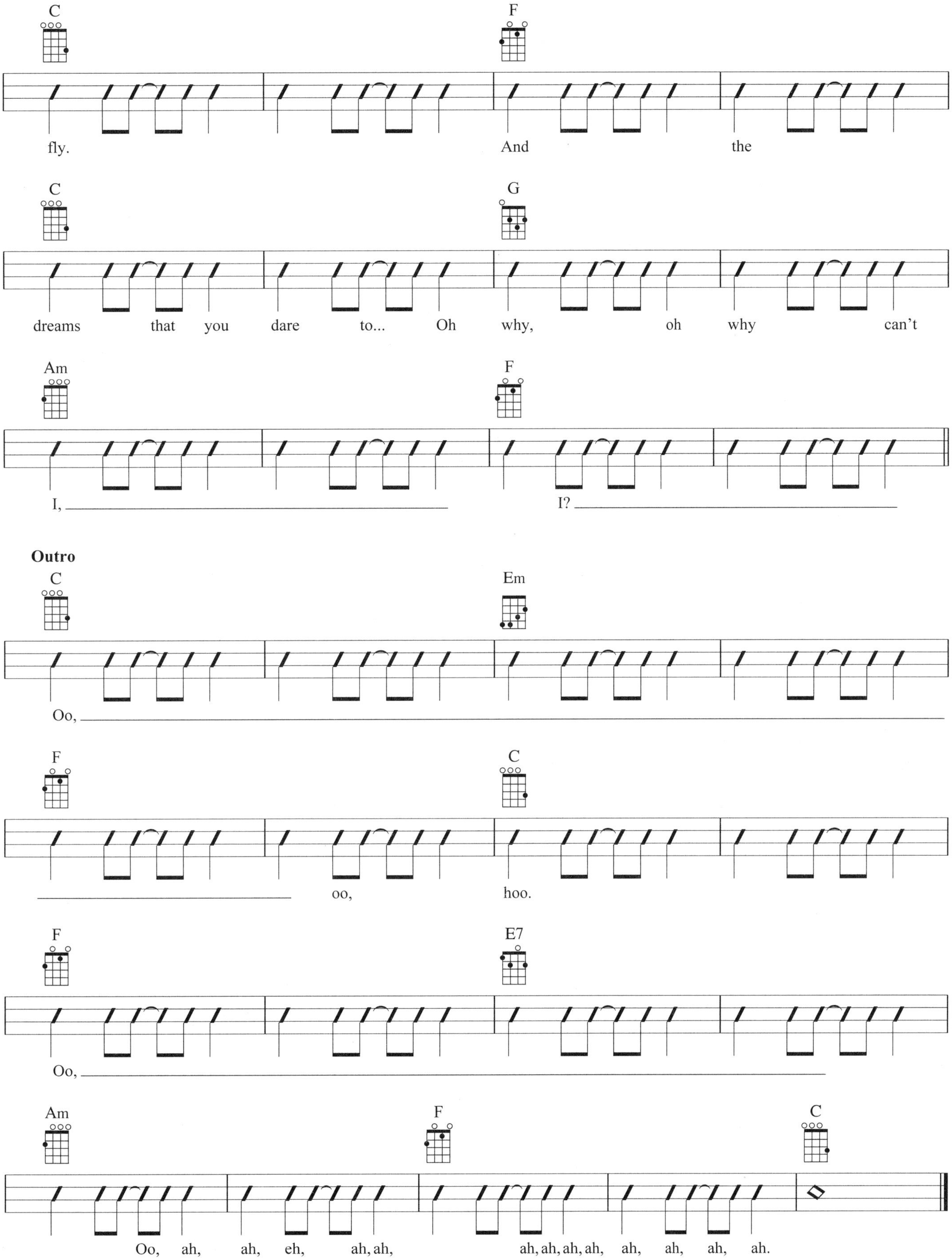
C
F
fly.
And
the
C
G
dreams that you dare to... Oh why, oh why can't
Am
F
I, I?
Outro
C
Em
Oo,
F
C
oo, hoo.
F
E7
Oo,
Am
F
C
Oo, ah, ah, eh, ah, ah, ah, ah, ah, ah, ah, ah, ah, ah.

CHAPTER 6

Barre Chords

A *barre chord* (pronounced "bar chord") involves using your fretting hand to hold down two or more strings on the same fret with just one finger. With the chords we've learned so far, it's been important to fret with just our fingertips, but when playing a barre chord, we need to lay one finger flat.

To play the B♭ barre chord, lay finger 1 flat to cover both string 1 and 2. (**Note:** In a chord diagram, a barre is shown with a curved line connecting the notes to be barred.) It's often helpful to roll the finger a bit to the side, towards the headstock. After getting this finger in place, use the fingertips of fingers 2 and 3 to hold down the notes on strings 3 and 4, respectively. Study the chord diagram and photo to get a clear idea of what your fretting hand should look like. Once you have all of your fingers on the fretboard, play each note individually to make sure everything is ringing out clearly.

B♭

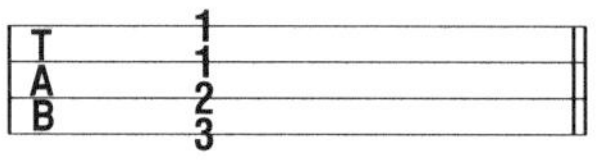

B♭

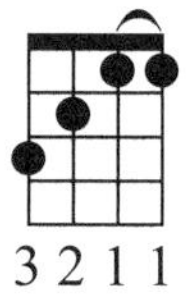

Don't fret (pun intended) if your barre chords don't sound good right away. They are tricky, and it may take some time to get them under your fingers. Keep at it and be patient!

Before we use the B♭ barre chord in the next song, we also need to learn two new chords that aren't barre chords, Dm and Gm.

Dm

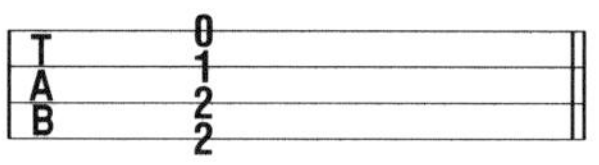

Dm

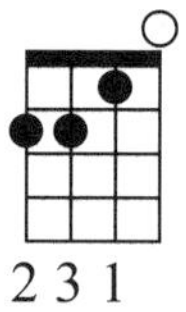

Gm

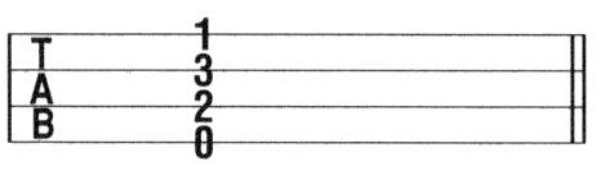

Gm

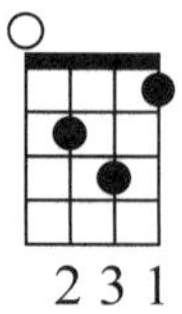

Dotted Quarter Notes

Let's talk about the first note in the next song, the *dotted quarter note*. Whenever a dot is added to a note, its value is increased by half. So, that dotted quarter note is worth 1 1/2 beats (as if you tied an eighth note to a quarter note). With this in mind, we can see that the second strum of the song doesn't hit until the "and" of beat two. Remember, you can always count "**one**-and, **two**-and, **three**-and, **four**-and" to help figure out where the eighth-note strums line up. In "All of Me," we'll start off with a simple strumming pattern that includes tied notes and imitates the piano part. If you have trouble understanding the rhythm here, listen to the rhythm of the piano part in the original recording. For the pre-chorus and chorus, we'll use one of the popular strumming patterns that we learned in the previous chapter.

All of Me

Words and Music by John Stephens and Toby Gad

Pre-Chorus
Gm F C
right. My head's under water, but I'm breathing fine.
Gm F C
You're crazy and I'm out of my mind. 'Cause
Chorus
F Dm
all of me loves all of you. Love your
B♭ C
curves and all your edg - es, all your perfect im-per-fec - tions. Give your
F Dm
all to me, I'll give my all to you. You're my
B♭ C
end and my begin - ning. Even when I lose, I'm win - ning 'cause I give you all
Dm B♭ F C
of me. And you give me all
Dm B♭ F C
of you, oh.

Even though barre chords are super challenging, they offer a huge plus side: since they don't use any open strings, barre chords are movable. This means we can take that same B♭ shape we just learned and move it up one fret to play a B chord. (If we move it up one more fret, we have a C chord... and so on.) When you learn one barre chord shape, you can use that chord shape all over the neck to play other chords.

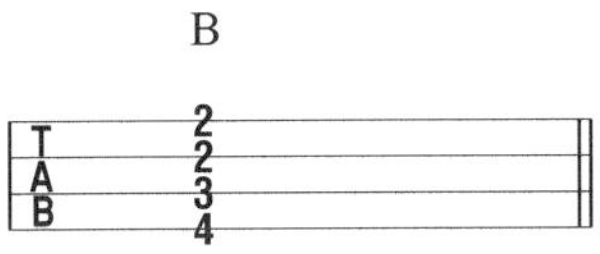

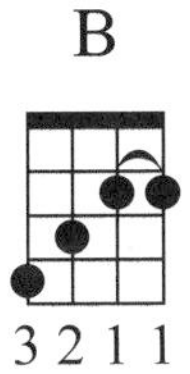

Can you recognize the chord shape that the F♯ barre chord is based on? It's our F chord moved up one fret! Here, a barre is used to move the open notes up one fret. Finger 4 or 3 may be used on string 4.

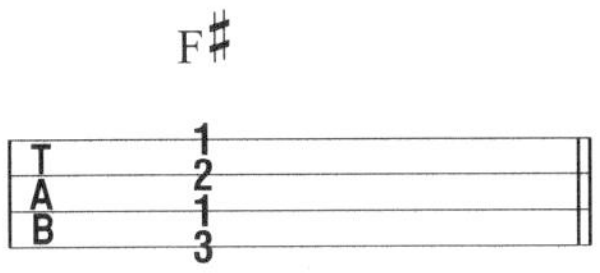

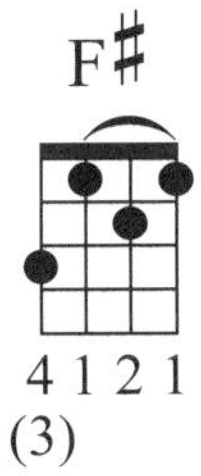

Before we use our new barre chords in a song, we need to learn a few more chords. The G♯m looks just like the Gm chord, except we've moved all the notes up one fret. The E chord is the same shape as the D chord, but all the notes are moved up two frets, including the open note.

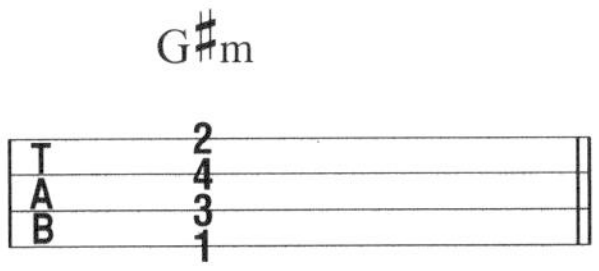

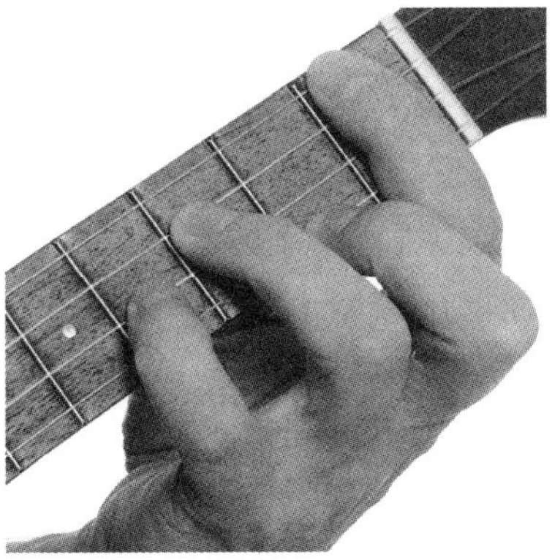

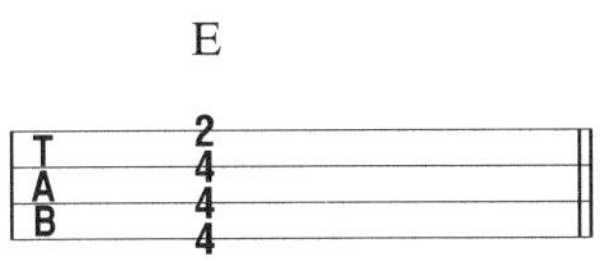

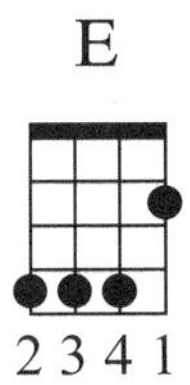

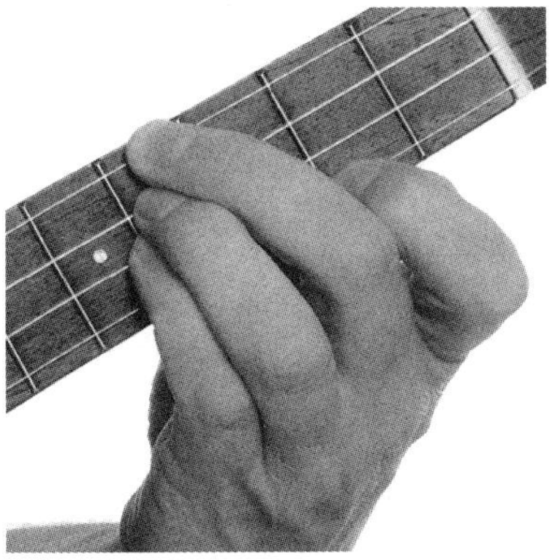

Sixteenth Notes

Finally, before we play the next song, we need to learn one more type of note, the *sixteenth note*. As you know, eighth notes go by twice as fast as quarter notes, so for every quarter note, we have two eighth notes. Well, sixteenth notes further divide the beat. It takes two sixteenth notes to equal one eighth note, and therefore four sixteenth notes to equal one quarter note. To track the sixteenth-note subdivision, count "**one**-e-and-a, **two**-e-and-a, **three**-e-and-a, **four**-e-and-a," with each syllable representing one sixteenth note. Try counting along with the following rhythm exercise, alternating between downstrokes and upstrokes as shown.

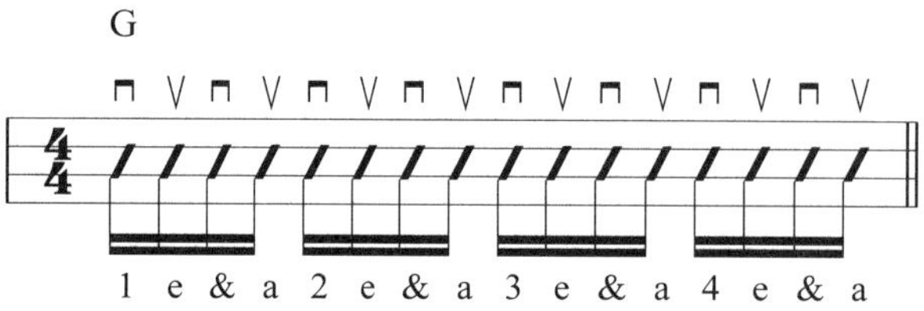

The strumming pattern we'll use for "I'm Yours" will include a combination of eighth notes and sixteenth notes. If you have trouble figuring out how it should sound, say the word "coconut" four times for each measure and match your strumming to the syllables.

I'm Yours

Words and Music by Jason Mraz

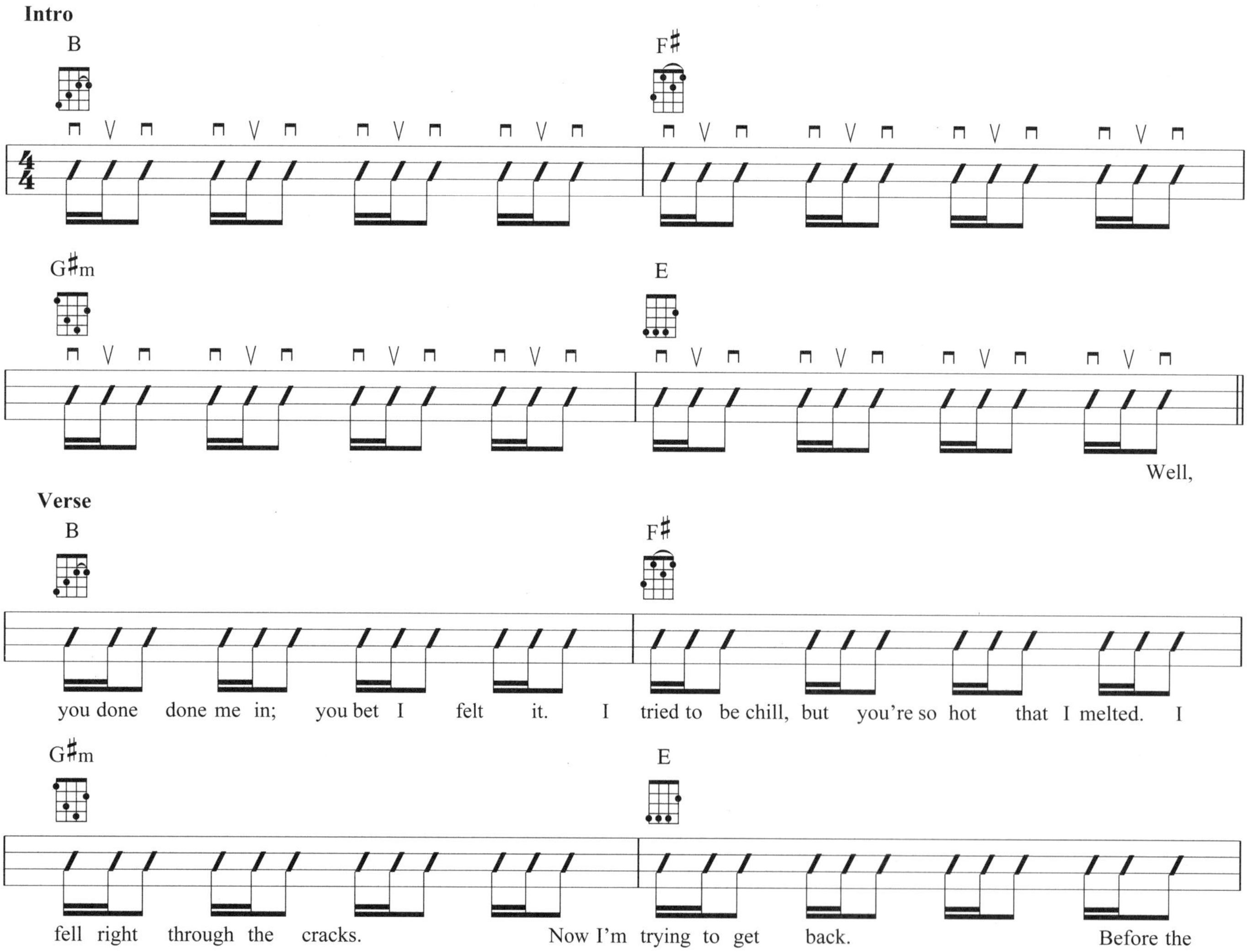

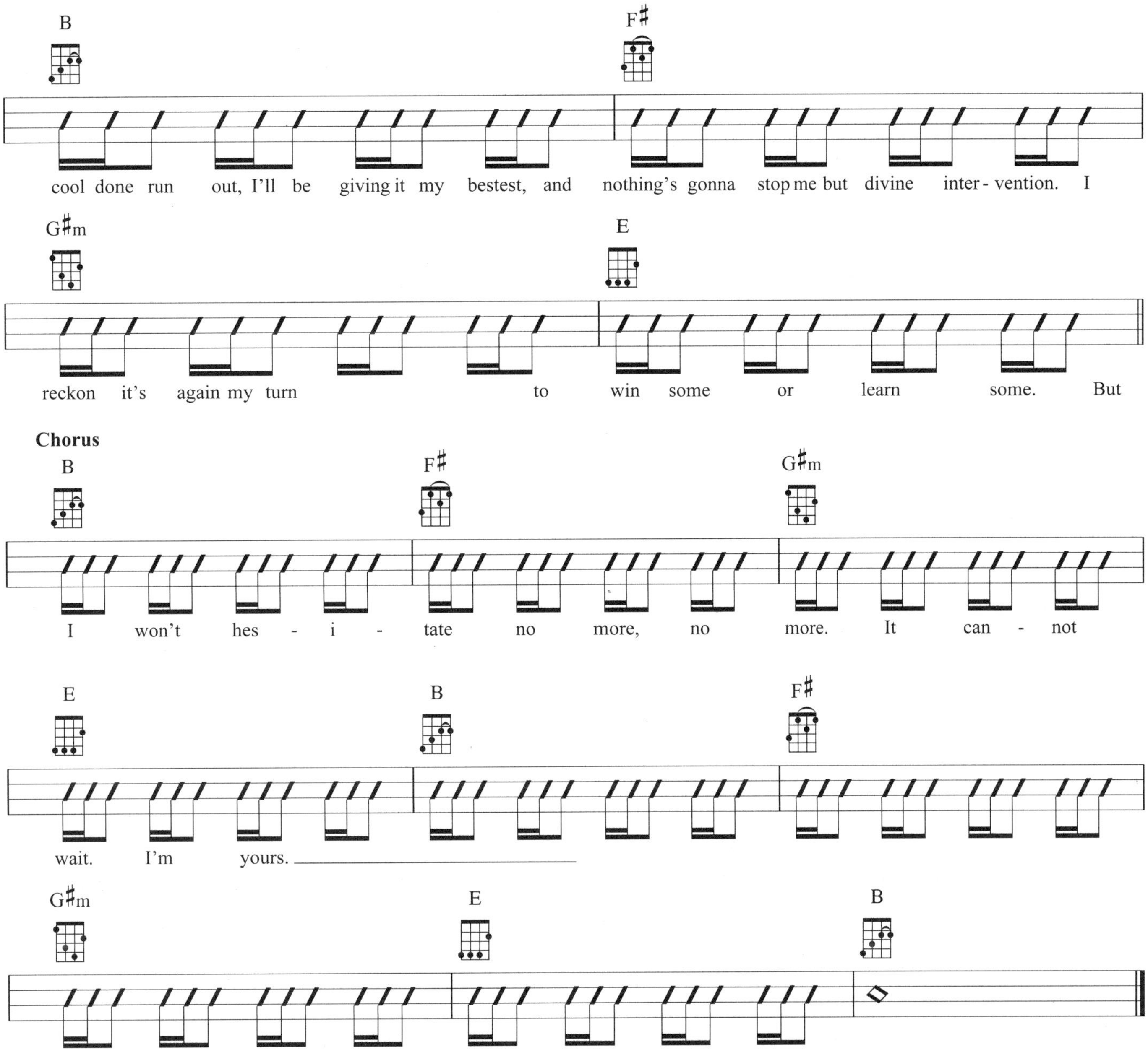

We'll conclude this chapter on barre chords with a bona fide ukulele hit, "Hey, Soul Sister" by Train. While many of the other songs in this book have simply been well suited to a ukulele arrangement, "Hey, Soul Sister" features a ukulele as the main instrument! Before we play it, though, we'll need to learn another new barre chord, C♯m. To play this barre chord, use finger 1 to cover strings 1–3 at the 4th fret. (**Note:** The "4fr" marking in the chord diagram indicates that our chord shape starts at the 4th fret, not down by the nut as usual.)

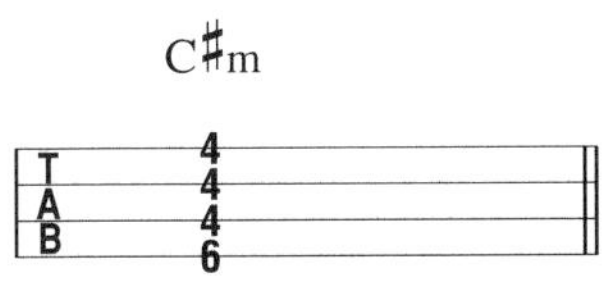

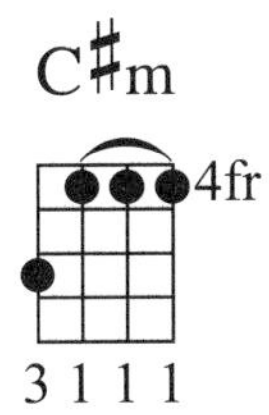

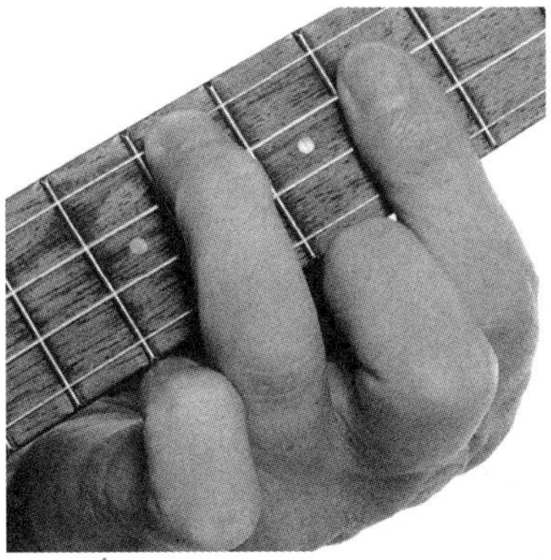

In this song, we'll again be using sixteenth notes in our strumming pattern. As always, start out slowly until you feel comfortable with the rhythm. If you're confused about where the strums fall, try saying the phrase "piz-za pep-peroni" twice for each measure, matching your strums to the syllables of the words: "**down**-down, **down**-up-down-up, **down**-down, **down**-up-down-up." You might want to practice the quick chord changes in the second measure of the chorus before playing the whole thing straight through. On the repeat, sing the second verse of lyrics.

Hey, Soul Sister

Words and Music by Pat Monahan, Espen Lind and Amund Bjorklund

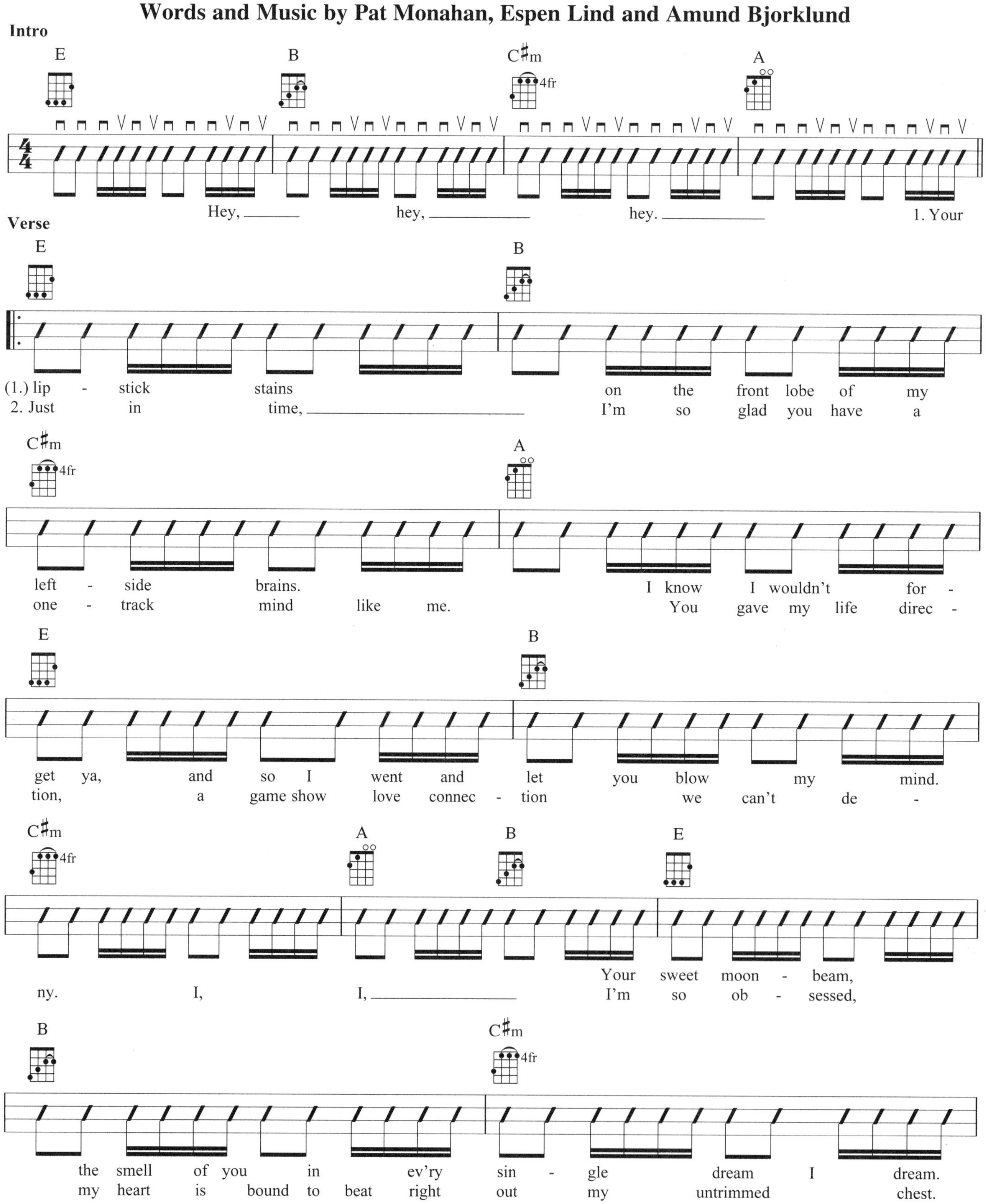

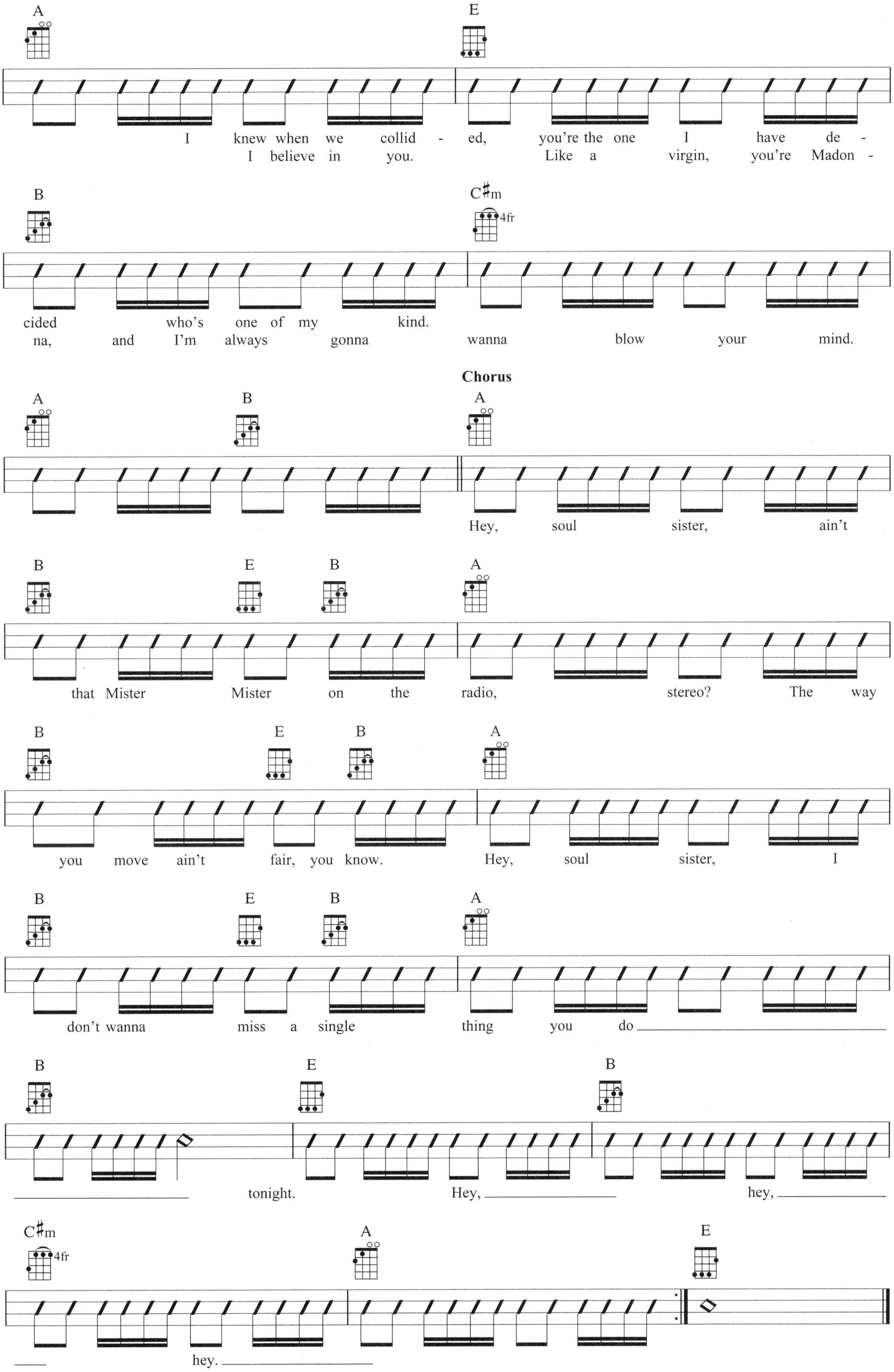
A
E
I knew when we collid - ed, you're the one I have de -
I believe in you. Like a virgin, you're Madon -
B
C♯m
4fr
cided who's one of my kind.
na, and I'm always gonna wanna blow your mind.
Chorus
A
B
A
Hey, soul sister, ain't
B
E
B
A
that Mister Mister on the radio, stereo? The way
B
E
B
A
you move ain't fair, you know. Hey, soul sister, I
B
E
B
A
don't wanna miss a single thing you do
B
E
B
tonight. Hey, hey,
C♯m
4fr
A
E
hey.

CHAPTER 7

Combining Chords with Melody

Solo Arrangements

Early on in the book, we learned to play single-note melodies. Then, we focused on chords for strumming and playing accompaniment with vocals. Now we're going to talk about how we can combine those two approaches to create what are referred to as *solo arrangements*. With this type of an arrangement, a song played by one person can sound full and complete. We add some *harmony* (extra notes) to the melody, and often fill in the holes in the melody by strumming chords; with everything going on, these arrangements tend to be more challenging. In the songs we'll look at, some chords you'll recognize, and some will be new, so use the included chord diagrams along with everything you've learned so far to master these new chords. Playing tips for each song are included, providing details about how best to learn and practice the arrangements, but the lyrics to these songs have been intentionally left out so that you can focus on the challenging ukulele parts.

The only new chord we need to know to play our first solo arrangement is D7, formed by laying down finger 1 as a barre across the 2nd fret and adding finger 2 to string 1 on the 3rd fret.

D7

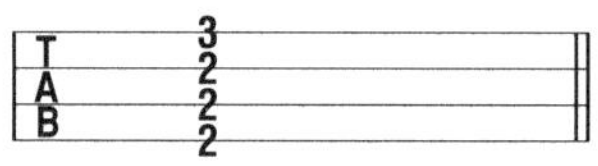

D7

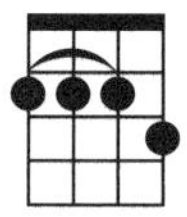

The first solo arrangement we'll look at is "Every Breath You Take" by the Police. After the strummed intro, the arrangement starts off with a simple single-note melody, and then we start filling in the gaps with some chord strumming. You'll recognize the strumming pattern, as we've already used it a couple of times. In general, it will be easiest to use your thumb to strum the melody notes and single chords, but if you find a different option that works better for you, go for it!

Every Breath You Take

Music and Lyrics by Sting

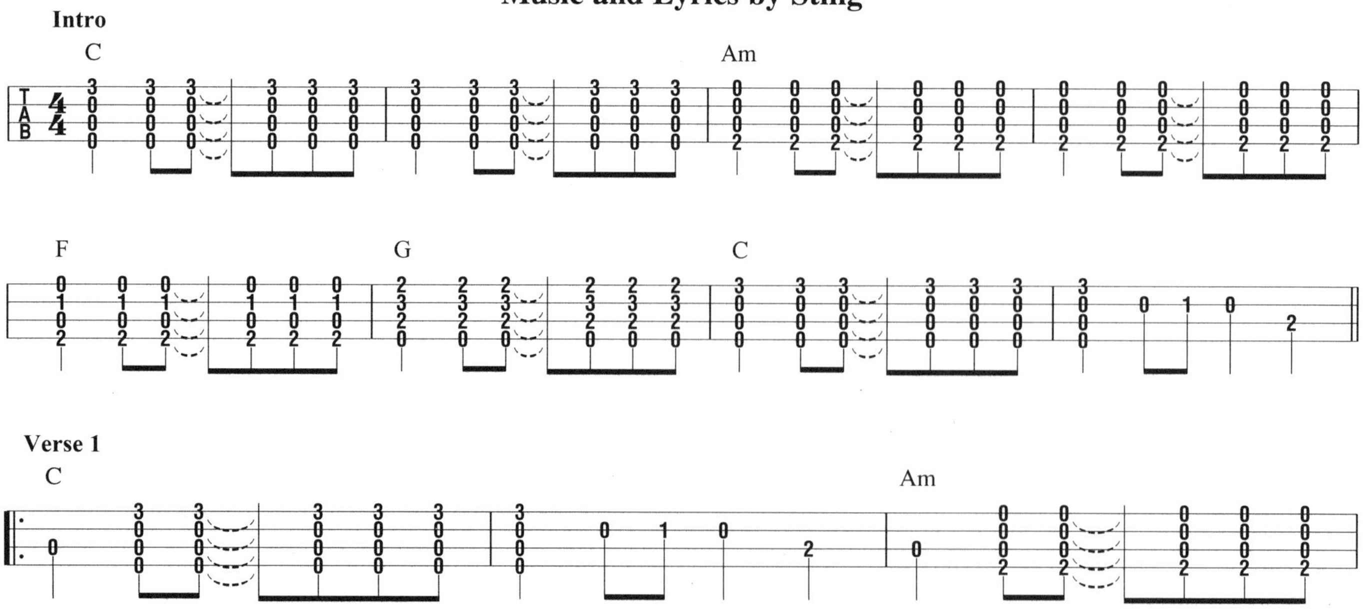

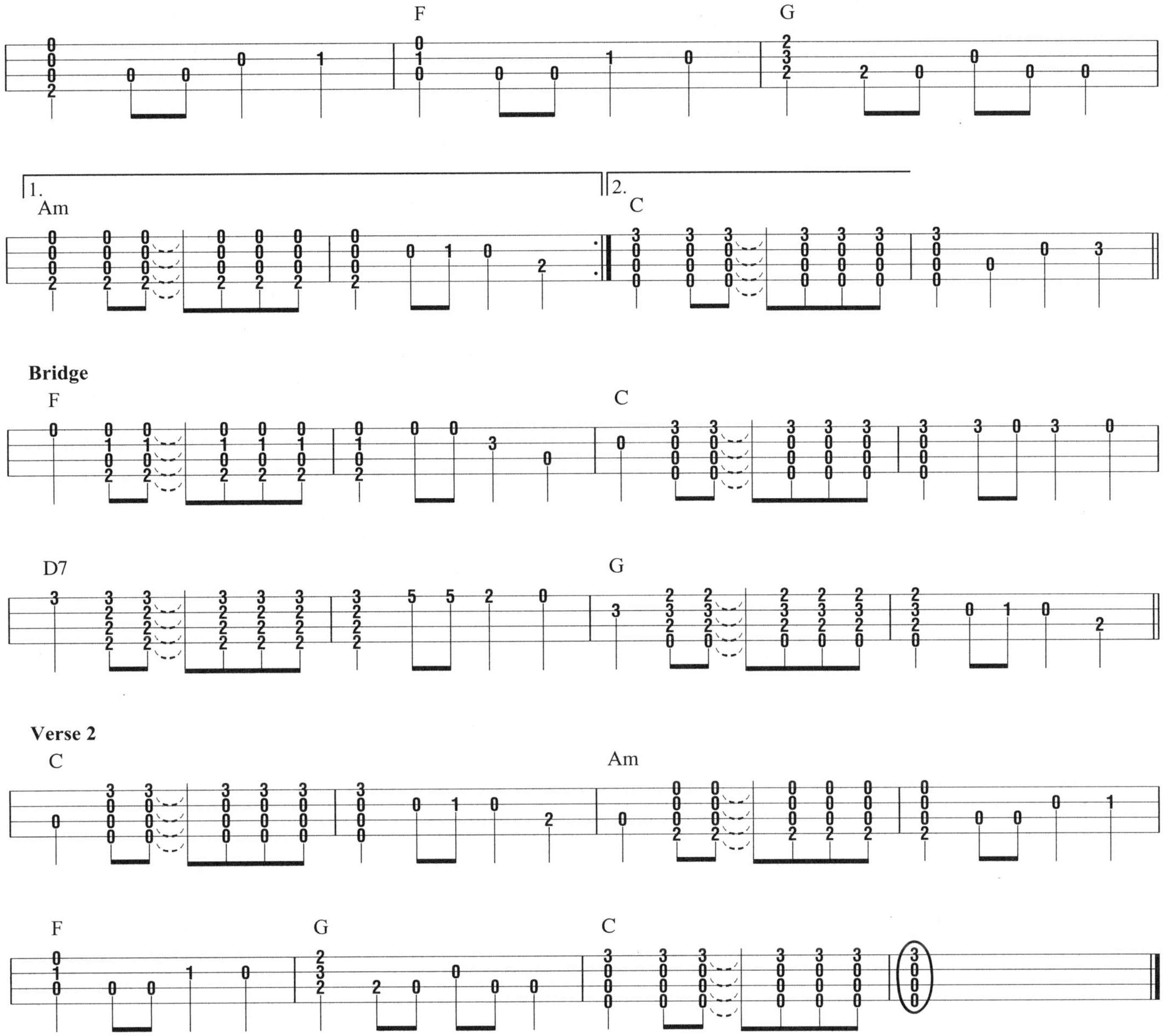

Chord Voicings

For the next tune, "Can't Help Falling in Love," we'll learn a new fingering for a chord we already know, the E7 chord. Notice that the shape and fingering of this E7 is the same as D7, but it's moved up two frets—remember, that's the beauty of the movable barre chord!

E7

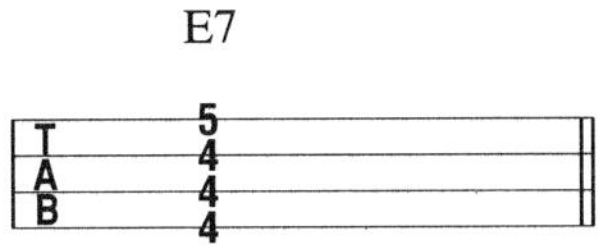

E7

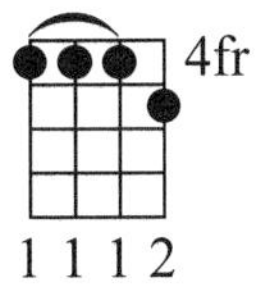

You might be wondering how and why we have different fingerings for the same chord. Well, first off, chords must have a certain combination of notes to be named as they are (e.g., C, E, G = C chord; G, B, D, = G chord; E, G♯, B, D = E7 chord). However, we can use any combination of these notes to form the chords. As long as we have the right notes within the chord, the chord will still be called by the same name regardless of how the notes are arranged or where we play them on the fretboard (e.g., C, E, G = C chord; E, G, C = C chord; G, C, E = C chord). When we put the notes of a chord in a different order, that chord is said to be using a new *voicing*. In the case of the first version of E7 that we learned, we had the notes G♯, D, E, and B, in that order. But for this next version of the E7 chord, the order of the notes is B, E, G#, and D. So, as you can see, the two chord shapes use the same notes, just in a different order. Why would we want to use a different voicing for any of the chords in this song? It has to do with finding good chord shapes that will allow you to put the melody notes on the top the chords. Yes, we could use the old E7 chord in this song, but since we want the D melody note to stand out at the top of the E7 chord, this new E7 chord works perfectly.

Triplets

In our next song, you'll notice a bracketed number "3" below some of the notes. This tells us that these notes are part of a triplet. In its simplest explanation, a *triplet* is a grouping of three notes that's played in the space where you normally would play two, and depending on how it's shown, a triplet will fill the space of either a single beat or two beats. Here, the triplet is played in the space of two beats. If you sing the line "fal-ling in," which follows the lyric "but I can't help," you should feel that triplet just fine! (**Note:** When a triplet is meant to be played over just one beat—which is perhaps more common than the two-beat triplet we have here—it normally won't include a bracket, and instead you'll see what looks like three connected eighth notes with a "3" by the beam.)

In verse 1 of "Can't Help Falling in Love," the highest note of each chord will be the melody note. Then, in verse 2, we'll play the melody notes followed by a chord or two for accompaniment. This changes the feel a bit and adds some variation. During the bridge, use finger 2 on the 5th fret of string 1. This will allow you to keep holding that finger down when moving to the E7 chord. Also, notice that we're sometimes strumming partial chords, which is another way that we can put a melody note on the top of a chord.

Can't Help Falling in Love

Words and Music by George David Weiss, Hugo Peretti and Luigi Creatore

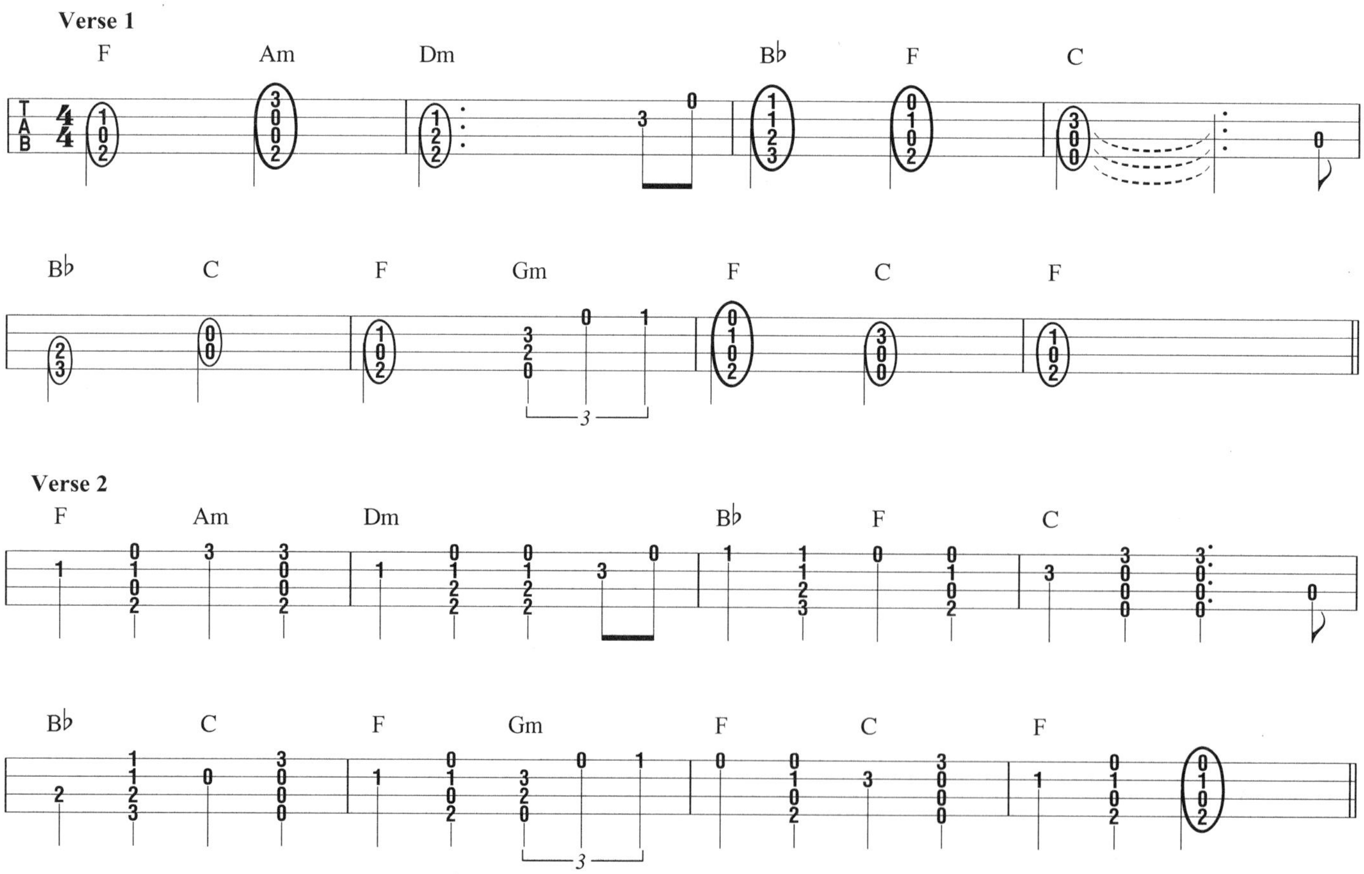

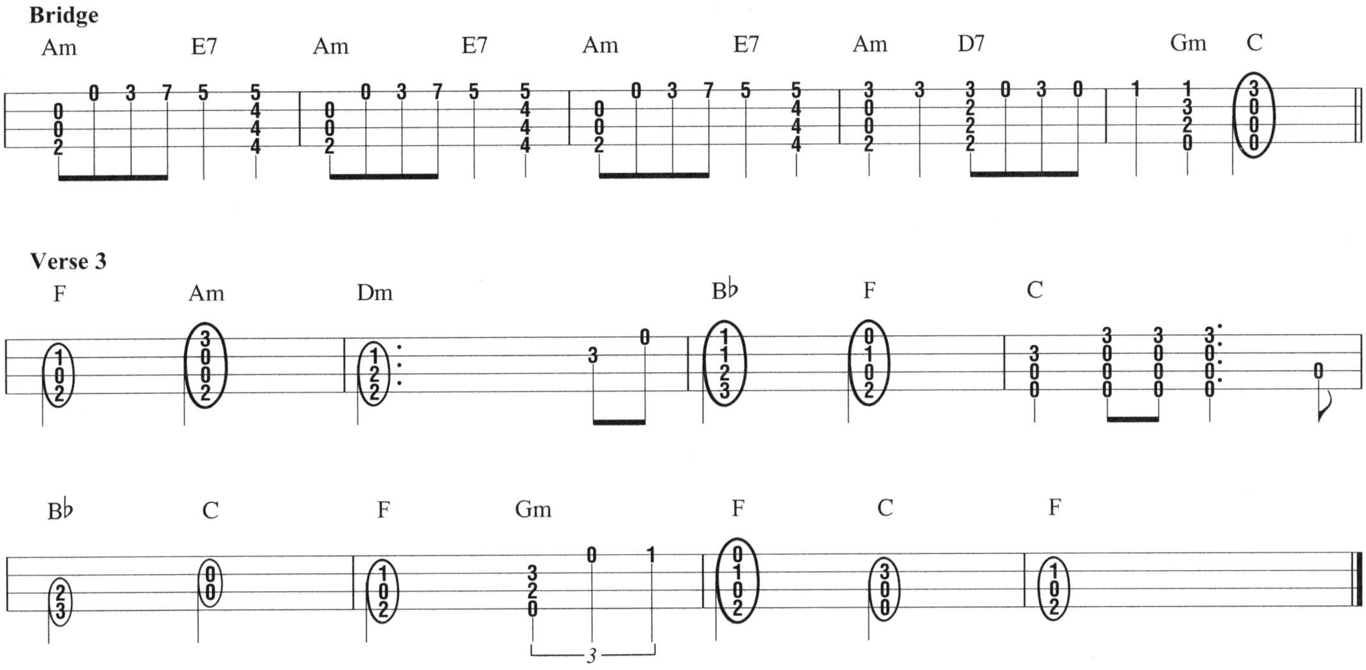

In our next song, “Silent Night,” we’ll be playing two new voicings of the G7 chord. Again, this is to help put the melody note on the top of the chord. You should recognize the second G7 voicing as a D7 moved up to the 7th fret.

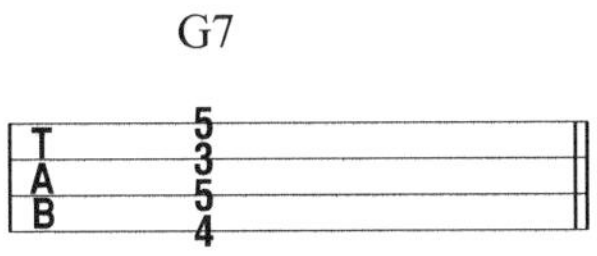

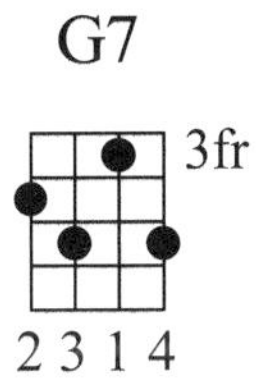

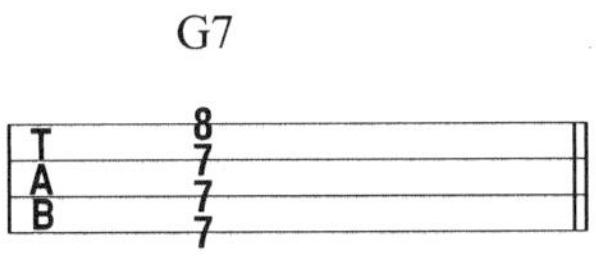

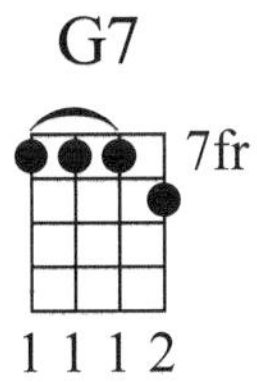

In this arrangement, you’ll start almost every measure by playing a chord that contains the melody note on top, followed by some single melody notes. We’ll also use string 4 for a few melody notes. You can either strum and pluck every single chord and note with the thumb, or you can try using the index or middle finger on the right hand for the notes on string 1 and the thumb for everything else. In the first measure, hold down the chord for the whole measure to easily come back to that last melody note in the measure. (Always look for ways like this to play a song more efficiently.) To play the note on the 3rd fret of string 1 in measure 10, we can simply add finger 4 to the chord we played in measure 9. Also, don’t be confused if you see a particular chord name listed above the music but you’re not playing the full chord. The chord names represent the harmony of the song, and sometimes we need to grab only certain notes of the chord to fit in the melody note correctly.

Silent Night

Words by Joseph Mohr
Translated by John F. Young
Music by Franz X. Gruber

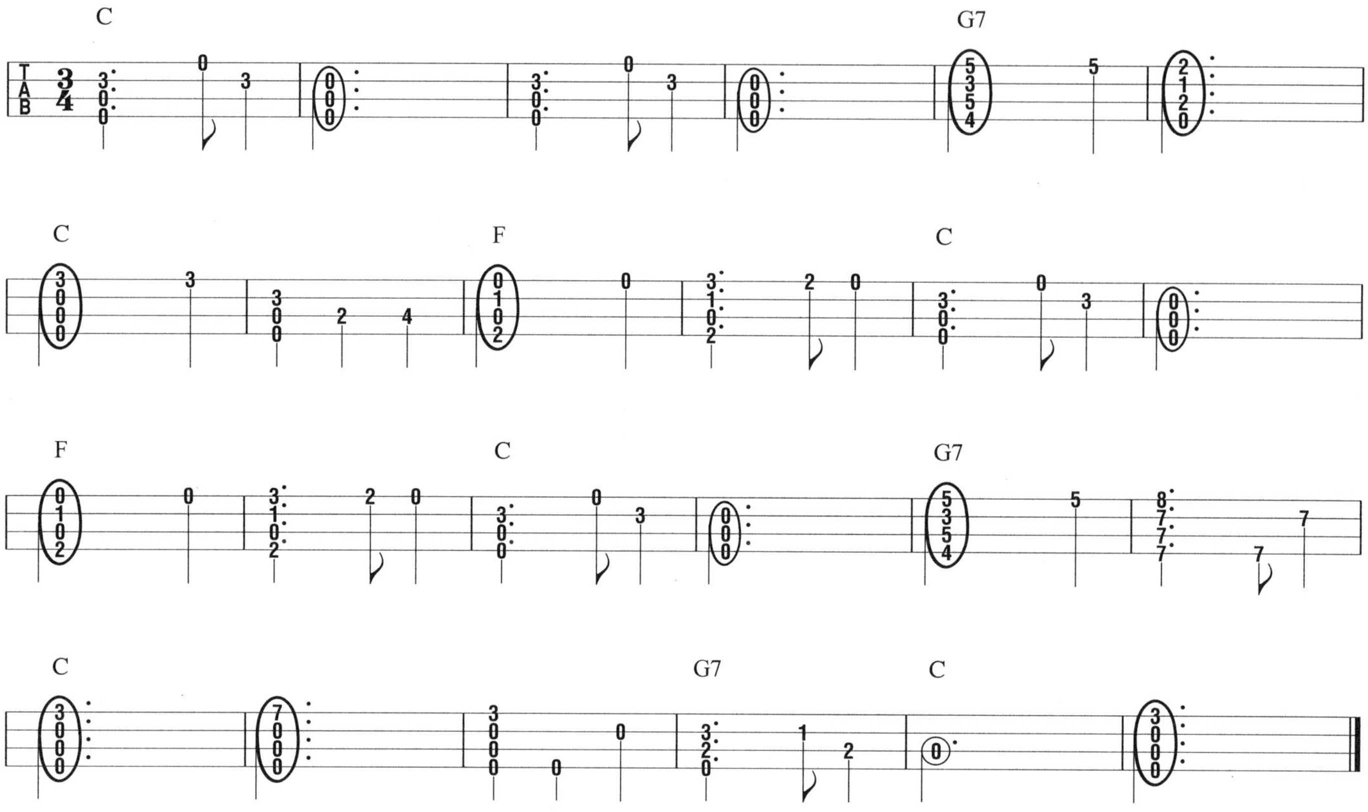

For our final song, we'll look at the Beatles classic "Yesterday." First off, let's check out some of the new chords we'll need. The A7sus4 chord sounds complicated, but it's actually super easy. Just one finger! As always, make sure you're fretting chords like this with your fingertips, so all the open notes are ringing.

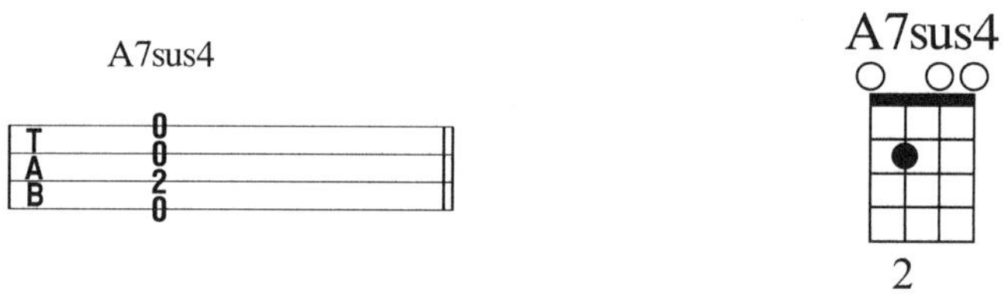

Next up is an A7 chord. You should recognize that the shape looks a lot like a G chord, and you might be asking yourself, "If we move a G chord up two frets, shouldn't it just be an A chord?" Well, since we left string 4 open and didn't also raise that note, it's not operating like a movable barre chord; not all of the notes were moved up, so the combination of notes is not the same. Leaving that open string in the mix gives this chord the note combination that makes up an A7 chord.

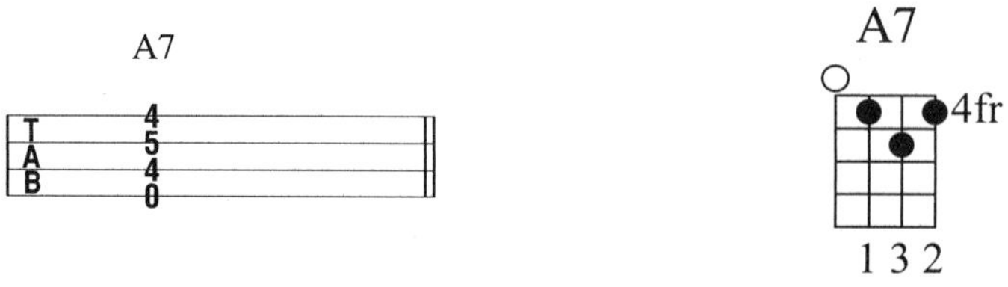

Here's the Dm9 chord, another movable barre chord. The Dm7 chord is formed by barring all four strings at the 5th fret.

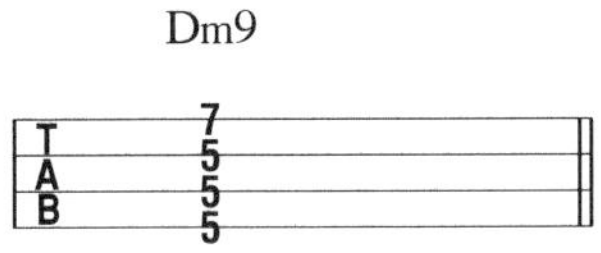

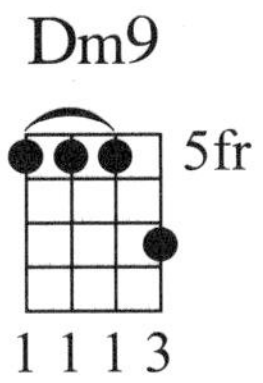

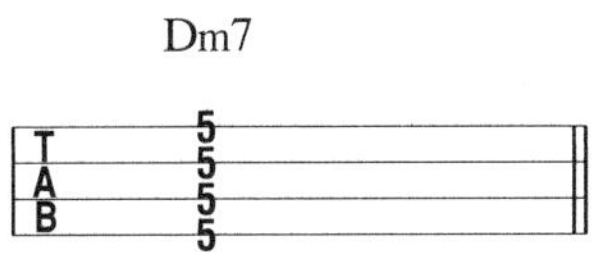

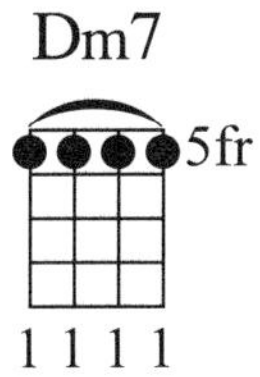

Here's a really easy version of an A7 chord, and another easy version of a C chord.

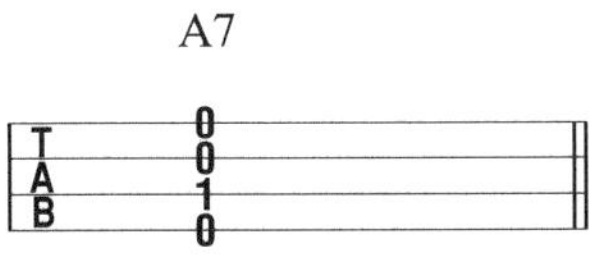

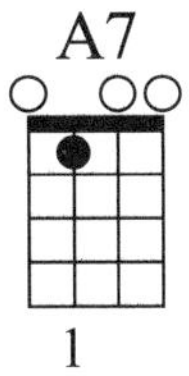

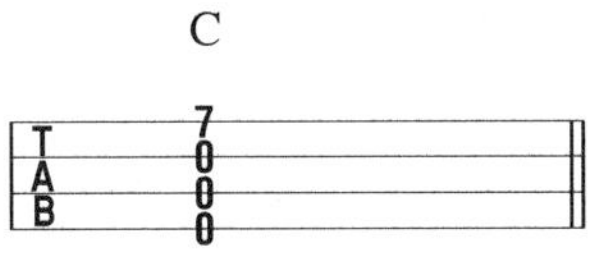

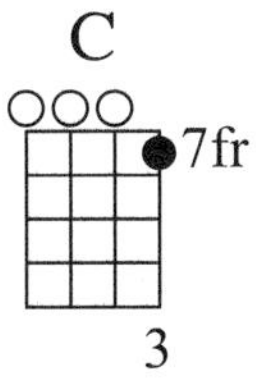

B♭5 only includes two notes, B♭ and F. When we play it on three strings, we just add the F in the next octave up to give the chord a fuller sound. Remember that whenever you see an "X" above a string in a chord diagram, as we see here, it means you should not play that string at all.

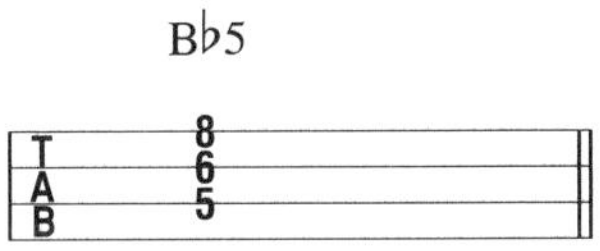

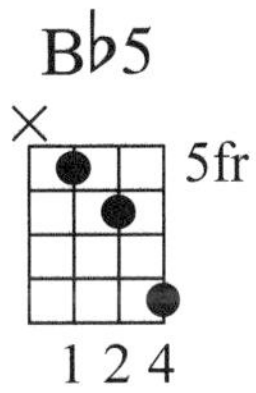

Finally, we have a movable barre-chord version of an F chord up on the 5th fret.

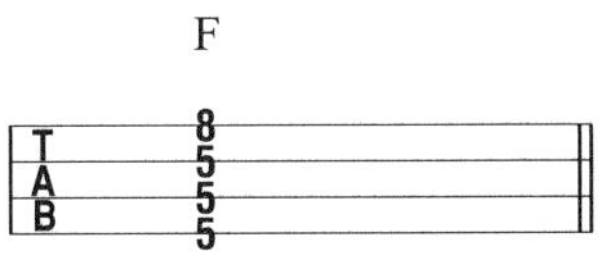

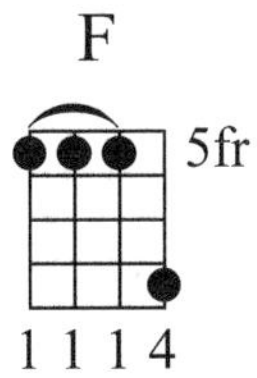

That's a lot of new chords to learn! So, it will be helpful to practice forming and moving between them a bit before tackling the solo arrangement.

The intro to "Yesterday" starts with some basic strumming of an F chord. For the verse, we're playing chord-melody lines along with accompaniment strumming. When you get to the Dm9 chord, leave the barre down for the entire measure in order to play the melody notes on the 5th fret that follow the chord strum. In the fourth measure of each verse, note how we again use the open string 4 for a melody note; while that string is not used often for melody notes, it sometimes can come in handy to make playing a melody line easier. The second measure of the bridge includes some fast-moving chords, so you may want to practice that section separately until those changes flow easily. In general, you can use the thumb for plucking melody notes and for strumming chords containing melody notes, but for any repeated strumming, try using the first finger.

Yesterday

Words and Music by John Lennon and Paul McCartney

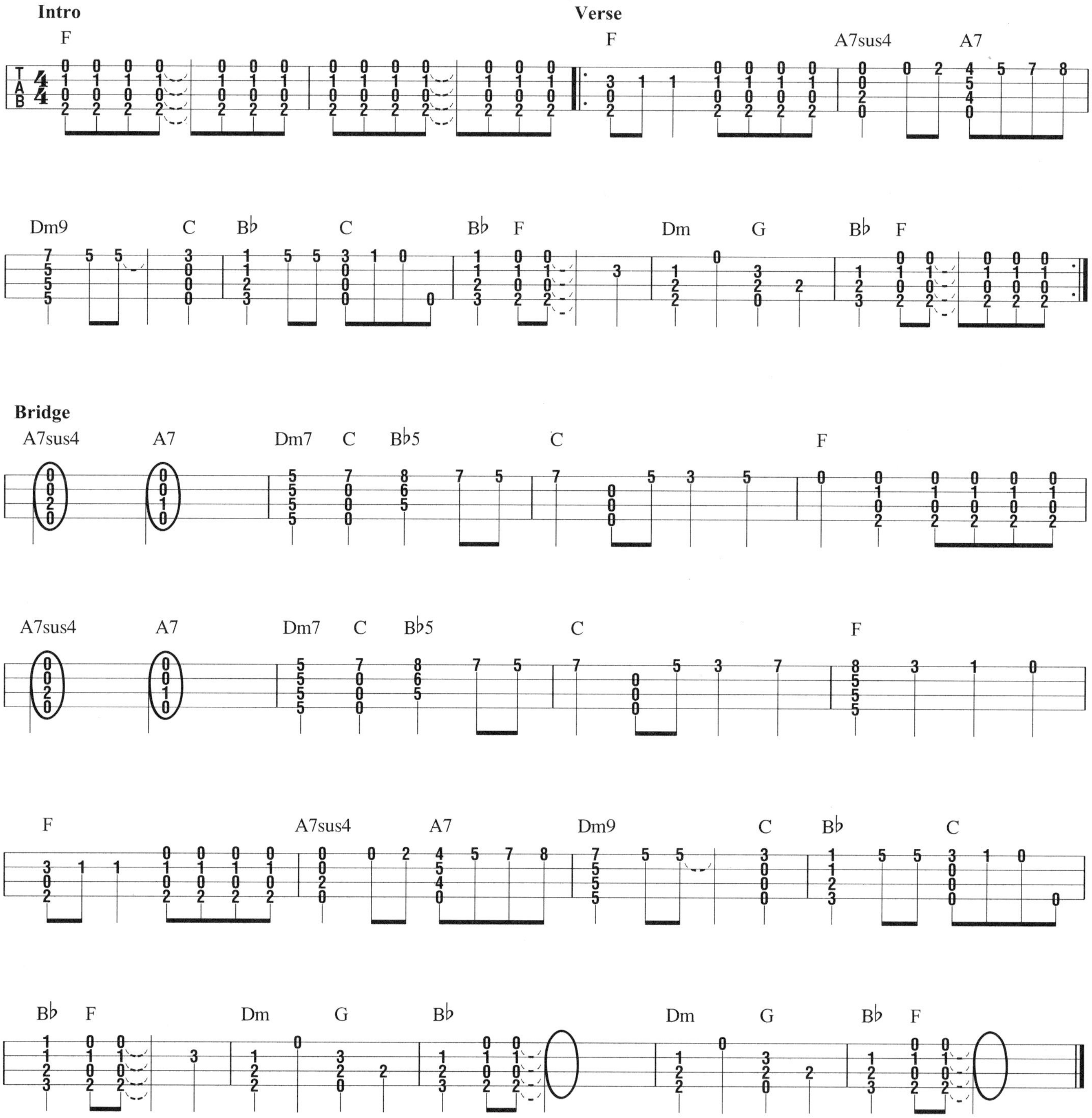

Closing Note

Congratulations on teaching yourself to play the ukulele! Even though this is the end of the book, it's not the end of your journey. There's always more to learn—new chords, new songs, new techniques—and it's always a great idea to continue playing the songs you've already learned. Don't practice something until you get it right; practice it until you can't play it wrong. Again, above all, have fun and enjoy your musical journey!